ARCHAEOLOGICAL SURVEY OF WESTERN INDIA, VOL. VI

ON THE
MUHAMMADAN ARCHITECTURE
OF
BHAROCH, CAMBAY, DHOLKA, CHAMPANIR, AND MAHMUDABAD IN GUJARAT,

ARCHAEOLOGICAL SURVEY OF WESTERN INDIA, VOL. VI

ON THE
MUHAMMADAN ARCHITECTURE
OF

BHAROCH, CAMBAY, DHOLKA, CHAMPANIR, AND MAHMUDABAD IN GUJARAT,

BY

JAS. BURGRESS, C.I.E., LL.D., F.R.S.E.,
HON. A.R.I.B.A., F.R.G.S., M.R.A.S., M.SOC. AS. PARIS;
HON. COR. MEM. BERLIN SOC. OF ANTHROPOLOGY, ETC., AND BAT. SOC. OF ARTS AND SCIENCES;
LATE DIRECTOR-GENERAL OF THE ARCHAEOLOGICAL SURVEY OF INDIA.

GYAN

Published by

Gyan Publishing House
5, Ansari Road
Daryaganj, New Delhi-110002
Phone: 011-47034999, 9811692060
E-mail: books@gyanbooks.com

Distribution Network
gyanbooks.com
India, USA, Canada, UK, Australia, France

ISBN : 978-81-212-2866-4 (HB)
First Published, 1896

2nd Impression 2021

Printed at: Gyan Press, Delhi.

On the
Muhammadan Architecture
of
Bharoch, Cambay, Dholka, Champanir, and Mahmudabad in Gujarat
Author: Jas. Burgress

ARCHÆOLOGICAL SURVEY OF WESTERN INDIA, VOL. VI.

ON THE

MUHAMMADAN ARCHITECTURE

OF

BHAROCH, CAMBAY, DHOLKA, CHAMPANIR, AND MAHMUDABAD IN GUJARAT.

BY

JAS. BURGESS, C.I.E., LL.D., F.R.S.E.,

HON. A.R.I.B.A., F.R.G.S., M.R.A.S., M.SOC. AS. PARIS;
HON. COR. MEM. BERLIN SOC. OF ANTHROPOLOGY, ETC., AND BAT. SOC. OF ARTS AND SCIENCES;
LATE DIRECTOR-GENERAL OF THE ARCHÆOLOGICAL SURVEY OF INDIA.

LONDON:
WM. GRIGGS & SONS, LIMITED.
BERNARD QUARITCH; A. CONSTABLE & Co.;
KEGAN PAUL, TRENCH, TRÜBNER, & Co.; LUZAC & Co.
CALCUTTA: THACKER, SPINK, & Co. BOMBAY: THACKER & Co., LIMITED.

1896,

TOMB OF MUBARAK SAYYID, AT SOJALI NEAR MAHMUDABAD.

PREFACE.

THE present volume is one—and the smaller one—of two in which the Muhammadan architecture of what may be described as the more important provincial towns of Gujarât is illustrated. The larger one deals almost exclusively with the capital—Aḥmadâbâd—and its suburbs. The two will thus, together, present a pretty comprehensive view of the Muslim remains in the British districts of Gujarât.

Among the many varieties in the style of Muhammadan architecture prevailing in different provinces of India, that which arose in Gujarât in the fourteenth and fifteenth centuries is one of the most instructive and deserving of study, as it is also the most beautiful. Like the Sharqi architecture of Jaunpur, it bears a markedly local impress, while the elements which compose it are of even a better and higher class than are to be found in any part of Gangetic India. Into any detailed examination of these elements it is not intended here to enter; the other volume will present a more suitable opportunity for remarks on this subject. Though there are not to be found at Aḥmadâdâd any such early examples as at Bharoch, Cambay, and Ḍholkâ, we have in that city a more consecutive series of buildings illustrative of the development of the style from the beginning of the fourteenth century when it began to take distinctive form and character till the seventeenth when it had begun to decay,—or, at least, when the erection of new buildings of importance architecturally had ceased to be undertaken by the Muhammadans.

The illustrations in this volume, however, present in sufficient detail the earlier Muslim mosques—erected at Bharoch and other towns on the overthrow of the Hindu power by the Moghuls from Dehli in the early part of the fourteenth century. As showing the first examples of the style, they will be found of much interest by anyone setting himself patiently to study the evolution and growth of so beautiful a form of Art; indeed such illustrations are indispensable for any such purpose.

Descriptions of the many details represented in the plates would have greatly expanded the letterpress; but the architectural student will be as well pleased when left to study the drawings and photographs themselves. The drawings are the work of native draftsmen, trained in the Survey, and were all made under the careful personal supervision of Mr. Henry Cousens, my then assistant, or of myself; they have only been reduced by photolithography.

JAS. BURGESS.

Edinburgh, November 1896.

CONTENTS.

a 4

THE

ARCHÆOLOGICAL SURVEY OF WESTERN INDIA.

THE MUHAMMADAN ARCHITECTURE

OF

GUJARÂT.

CHAPTER I.

GUJARAT.—HISTORICAL.

GUJARÂT may be roughly defined as the northern division of the Bombay Presidency, and its principal city Aḥmadâbâd lies about 280 miles in a straight line north from Bombay. The former limits of the province may be approximately marked out thus:—bounded on the north by the Lunî river, 200 miles north from Aḥmadâbâd, thus including Sirohi and adjoining areas, which now belong politically to the Rajput state of Jodhpur; and on the east by the southern spurs of the Aravalli hills which separate it from Mewâr and Mâlwâ, and by a line not very well defined, but which runs pretty nearly along the 74th meridian across the valleys of the Narmadâ and Tâptî, and then along the northern ridge of the Sahyâdri or Western Ghâṭs, separating it from Khandesh and Nâsik districts; on the south it is narrow and the boundary may be drawn at Daman, 180 miles south of Aḥmadâbâd. On the west the seaboard forms a very irregular line,—the gulf of Cambay or Kambhât lying between the mainland and the large peninsula of Soraṭh or Kâṭhiâwâḍ, which is included between the gulfs of Kambhât and Kachh. Lastly, the Raṇ of Kachh bounds Gujarât on the north-west as far as the river Lunî. Over all this area, about as large as Great Britain,—and even beyond its limits,—the race and language are the same.

The northern districts of Gujarât, outside the Bombay Presidency and the states under its control, are now usually spoken of as part of Rajputana; the rest of the area comprises the rich collectorates or zillas of Surat, Bharoch, Kheḍâ, and Aḥmadâbâd, the Pañch Mahâls districts, and the native states of Barodâ, Pâlanpur, Cambay, and numerous others in the peninsula and on the mainland, chiefly along the eastern border.

All along the eastern frontier it is hilly or bordered by hills—many of them of very considerable height. Between these and the coast line the country is flat or undulating; but the Kâṭhiâwâḍ peninsula is largely diversified by hills,—among which are the Chamardî hills near the site of the ancient capital of Valabhî; the almost isolated Śatruñjaya to the south of them, where the Jains have from time immemorial been engaged in covering the summits with temples to their Tîrthaṁkaras. Still further south is the solitary Talâjâ hill, and that of Sânâ west from it, both perforated with early Buddhist caves. Running across much of the south of the peninsula is the Gîr range long famous for its lions, and at the west extremity of which is Gîrnâr, 3600 feet high, the ancient Urjayata or Revatâchala, at the foot of which, in early times, the emperor Aśoka, the great patron of Buddhism, caused a copy of his famous edicts to be engraved on a granite rock. And to the south-west of Girnar are the Baradâ and other groups of hills.

The population consists of several distinct elements. In the peninsula—the Saurâshṭra of early times—the Âbhiras or the Âhîrs have formed one of these elements from a very early date—the Greek geographers speaking of Syrastrene as the coast of Abiria. The aboriginal Kolis, Bhills, and Mehers are still numerous in the plains and eastern hills; the fair Kâṭhîs are a later immigration from the Indus valley into the centre of the peninsula, to which they now give name; and Rajputs, Moghuls, and Marâṭhas have entered it at different periods and largely intermingled with or displaced the earlier settlers.

In early times the Peninsula of Saurâṣhṭra or Soraṭh was famed in Hindu legend as the retreat of Kṛishṇa and his Yâdavas when driven from Mathurâ by Jarâsandha the king of Magadha; here he built and fortified Dwârakâ, and at Prabhâsa, after a drunken brawl, in which his son Pradyumna and nearly all the Yâdava chiefs were killed, he was shot by the hunter Jaras—mistaking him for a deer. At Prabhâsa stood the famous temple of Somanâtha, the fame of which provoked one of Maḥmûd of Gaznî's great iconoclastic raids in 1025. The Buddhists had great establishments at Girnâr and various other places before the Christian era; and Girnâr, Śatruñjaya, Kambhâyat, and other sites have long been Tîrthas or sacred shrines and places of pilgrimage of the Jainas.

The coasts of Gujarât, too, were probably the parts of India best known to the early Alexandrian traders, and through them to the Greek and Roman geographers. Barygaza or Bharukachha, now Bharoch, was the great emporium of trade in ancient times with Arabia and the Red Sea, and continued to be so down to the time of the discovery of the Cape of Good Hope; and Nausâri, Supârâ, Kalyâṇa, with the coasts of Saurâshṭra and Kachh, were known to Ptolemy and the author of the *Periplus of the Erythræan Sea*.

In the first century of our era the Kshatrapa or Satrap dynasty seems to have obtained possession of Gujarât, probably with their first capital at Ujjain, for Ptolemy mentions that Tiastanes—the Chashṭana of the coins and inscriptions, and founder of the family—had his royal seat there; but the frequency of these mementos of his successors, in Kâṭhiâwâḍ would seem to suggest that they may have had a second capital and mint in Gujarât, and that they occasionally resided in the province. Their coins, which occur in great numbers, appear to be dated in the Śaka era and come down to about the close of the fourth century A.D., and we know that the country was conquered by Chandragupta in the first decade of the fifth century. The Gupta dynasty ruled by means of viceroys or Senâpatis, but about the end of the same century the senâpati Bhaṭârka threw off the yoke of his masters and established a new dynasty at Valabhî, not far from Siṅhapura or Sîhor. These rulers held Kâṭhiâwâḍ, Kachh, and the northern and eastern parts of Gujarât. Under them, and upon the decay and corruption of Buddhism, the Jainas seem to have succeeded in obtaining the favour of the secular power in the district, and for long afterwards they continued to be a numerous and influential class. Jainism here, possibly, occupied the shrines as well as the position of the dispossessed Buddhism, and rebuilt or transformed the older temples in honour of their Tîrthaṁkaras. On the decline of the Valabhis, Chaulukya rulers—possibly allied to the Chalukyas of the Kanarese districts—held sway in continental Gujarât.

The Valabhî dynasty is pretty well known to us from their land grants, engraved on copperplates, which have been found at Valâ and other places in the peninsula and in continental Gujarât. From these we know of a dynasty of some nineteen princes, ruling from about A.D. 485 to 765.

The Valabhî dynasty was probably overwhelmed by some raid of the early Muhammadans from Sindh. Tradition seems to point to this,[1] and Musalman history mentions that Junaid, son of 'Abdu'l Rahmân al Marrî, who was confirmed in the government of the Sindh frontier by the Khalif Hashâm bin 'Abdu'l Malik (A.D. 724), sent officers against Barûs (*i.e.* Bharoch), Ujjain, and other places and conquered *al Bailamân* and *Juzr* (Gujarât).[2] This was in the time of Śilâditya IV. of Valabhî (cir. A.D. 710–740); but the so-called conquests were of no duration, and were very soon all lost. The power of the Valabhî dynasty, however, was weakened and a later invasion—possibly under 'Amrû bin Jamâl, in the time of Khalif al Mansûr (754–775) finally dispossessed them of the peninsula.

Towards the end of the seventh century northern Gujarât is said to have been under a râja Jayaśekhar, who ruled at Panchâsar, but he was defeated and slain by a king Bhûyaḍa, Bhûvaḍa, or Bhû-râja from Kanauj,[3] who held the country until a supposed posthumous son called Vanarâja—"Forest King"—set up as independent and ruled till A.D. 805. He founded the city of Aṇhilapâṭana or Aṇhilwâḍa on the Sarasvati, 64 miles north-west from Aḥmadâbâd and 18 west from Siddhapur, as his capital. This city afterwards rose to great importance and was known to the early Arab traders and geographers as Nahrvâlah,—now called Pâtan or Piran-Paṭṭana. It continued to be the capital of Gujarât for six hundred years, yet so completely was it despoiled in the fifteenth century, that D'Anville tried in vain to identify the site of Nahrvâlah, and could only conjecture that it may have stood where Aḥmadâbâd

[1] Tod (*Rajasthan*, vol. I. pp. 83, 217, 218) says the invaders were Scythic, probably Parthians from Minagara, and that the fall of Valabhî took place in A.D. 524; so Cunningham, *Arch. Sur. Ind.*, vol. II. p. 70; K. Forbes, *Râs* Mâlâ, vol. I. p. 21. The Valabhî dynasty, we now know, however, lasted for two hundred years after this—till well into the 8th century.

[2] The name *Bailamân* or *Bailâimân* is doubtful and not identified. Could it stand for "Balabhi"? The identification of *Juzr* and Gujarât might be questioned, as many of the Arab names bear but an imperfect resemblance to the Indian ones, but the mention of Bharoch, &c., shows that the raids were made in the direction of Gujarât. Abu Zaid makes Al Jorz or Al Juzr the same as Kanauj. Conf. Reinaud, *Relation des Voyages*, tom. I. p. 133, and tom. II. pp. 17, 127.

[3] The *Mirât-i Aḥmadî*, in some MSS. has Phûr-des, possibly, as Sir E. C. Bayley suggests, for Pûâr-râja, Râja Deva of Kanauj. But Mas'ûdî (cir. A.D. 915) says that *Baûrah*, *Bauürah* or *Bûḍa* was the title of the kings of Kanauj.

now is.[1] Tieffenthaler, however, speaks of Pâttan as a very ancient city, of which the old name was Nehrvâla; and this was also noticed by Rennell in the last century.[2]

The Chauḍâ or Châpotkaṭa dynasty is said to have been founded by Vanarâja in Saṁvat 802, and to have lasted under seven princes till A.D. 941.

These Châpotkaṭa or Chauḍâ princes could not have been very powerful. They do not seem to have had any claim to paramount authority; the Râṭhoḍs or Râshṭrakûṭas held the south of continental Gujarât; and the Chauḍâs were perhaps looked upon as feudatories to Kanauj, from which Vanarâja is said to have wrested his kingdom, but which probably occupied only the districts along the shores of the Raṇ of Kachh and not extending into what is now the British district of Aḥmadâbâd. The name of Râja Bhûyaḍa in the middle of their dynastic list, too, is the very title ascribed by early Muhammadan writers to the kings of Kanauj or Al-Jurz; and again in 941 the Chauḍâs were supplanted by Mûlarâja, whose father Râja was a prince from Kanauj, a son of the king Bhuvanâditya.

These Chauḍâ râjas have left few if any monuments, and the only copperplate grant yet known, is one ascribed to Vanarâja, and is a late forgery.

Mûlarâja, said to have been the sister's son of Sâmantadeva Cḥaghada, the last of the Chaudas, on whom he made war, and the latter being slain in the contest, Mûlarâja soon extended the dominion which he had thus secured. He subdued Soraṭh and Kachh and defeated the king of Lâṭa or of the northern parts of the Koṅkaṇ to the south of the Narmadâ. About 982[3] he was threatened by the Sapâdalakshîya râja of Śâkambharî or Sâmbhar from the north, and by an army sent by Tailapa-deva from the Dekhan. He retired to Kanthkoṭ in Kachh till the former should withdraw, and having succeeded in inducing him to do so, he issued from his stronghold to attack the forces of Tailapa, which he defeated slaying the general Bârapa. He built the temple of Mûleśvara at Maṇḍali and others, and founded the great Śaiva shrine, known as the Rudra-Mâla at Siddhapura, to the east of Aṇhilapura, but did not live to finish it,—possibly the work was stopped on the invasion of his kingdom and not afterwards resumed. He also invited Brahmans from Prayâg (now Allahâbâd), Kanyakubja or Kanauj, Gaṅgâdvâra, Bânâras, and other places in upper India, and settled them at Siddhapura, Siṁhapura, Stambhatîrtha (now Kambhât), and other towns, where their descendants are still known as Audîchyas or "northerners." During his long reign of fifty-five years he evidently fostered Śaivism, and at its close in 996 he abdicated in favour of his son Châmunda, the second Chaulukya king, and became a Śaiva devotee or Sannyâsin at Siddhapur.

His son Châmunda (996–1009) is said to have built wells and tanks, but left many such tasks unfinished. The Muslim was beginning to threaten India, and the chroniclers have not dwelt on his reign nor on that of his son Vallabharâja, who died of small-pox, six months after his accession, while invading Mâlwâ, it is said, to avenge an insult offered to his father, who had abdicated and gone on pilgrimage to Bânâras.

[1] *Eclaircissemens*, p. 74.

[2] Tieffenthaler, tome I. p. 385; Rennell's *Memoir of a Map of Hindustan*, 3rd ed. (1793), p. 227; and Conf. Pennant's *View of Hindustan*, vol. I. p. 55. Col. Tod, in 1822, claimed the credit of identifying the place, *Travels in West. India*. Albîrûnî (A.D. 973–1048) calls the city Anhalwârah: Reinaud, *Frag. Arab. et Pers.*, p. 111.

[3] *Arch. Sur. W. India*, vol. II. p. 193.

Durlabharâja (1009–1021), his brother, built temples and the Durlabha sarovar or lake, at Aṇahilapura, and was a quiet prince.

Bhîmadeva I. the son of Nâgarâja, a younger brother of Durlabha, now ascended the throne, an able and warlike prince. Maḥmûd of Gaznî had already made many forays into India, directed against the idol shrines where he was most certain of realising vast booty in gold and gems; and Gujarât contained one of the twelve great Śaiva Jyotîrliṅgas—the famous temple of Somanâtha, on the south coast of Soraṭh. Against it he was soon to direct a great expedition. In September 1024 Maḥmûd started from Gaznî with 30,000 cavalry besides volunteers, and marching to Multân, which he reached in a month, he organised an immense commissariat carriage of camels. Thence he proceeded first to Ajmer, and having captured it, he at once turned south along the skirts of the Aravalli hills to Aṇhilavâḍa, which he reached in six weeks from Multân and took by surprise. Bhîmadeva, unprepared and unable to cope with such a force of cavalry, followed at first the tactics of his great-grandfather Mûlarâja and retired to Kaṇṭhkoṭ in Kachh to collect his forces. Maḥmûd pressed on towards Somanâtha, but the Hindû king's army soon fell upon him, and it was with difficulty the Muslim invader preserved himself and his army. On Thursday 30th January 1025, Maḥmûd reached Somanâtha and next day assaulted the fort which was desperately defended, but on Saturday the assailants entered the place and slew mercilessly all they met, till but few were left alive. "Near the idol was a chain of gold to which bells were attached: the weight of it was 200 mâns." . . . "The worth of what was found in the temple exceeded two millions of *dînârs*—all of which was taken. The number of the slain exceeded fifty thousand."[1]

Maḥmûd now proceeded in pursuit of Bhîmadeva, who had taken refuge in a fortress surrounded by water—possibly at Gândhavi, a few miles north-east of Miyâni on the Kâthiâwâḍ coast. All who were found in the fort were put to the sword, leaving much spoil to the barbarous conqueror. Maḥmûd is said to have seriously proposed to take up his residence in Gujarât, but was dissuaded from it by his counsellors. The Muslim army now proceeded to Sindh, but suffered greatly in the desert, either from being misled by a Hindû guide or from Bhîmadeva and other chiefs hanging in the rear of Maḥmûd and driving him into it. Only after much privation did the army reach Multân on the 2nd April 1026, while Bhîma returned to Aṇhilavâḍa to resume his government. The puppet, Dabishalîm or Devishalîm, set up by the Muhammadans—probably at Somanâtha only,—was soon got rid of and all trace of Musalman authority destroyed.

The province had now rest from further invasion for a century and a half. In this period of respite were raised some of the finest Hindû and Jaina buildings in Gujarât,—notably the Jaina temple built by Vimala Sâh on Mount Abu in 1032, the Hindû and Jaina shrines on Mount Arasur, the great Rudramâla at Siddhapur, and the restored temple at Somanâtha. It was an age in which costly and elaborate sacred buildings were rising in great numbers all over the Dekhan, under the sway of the Châlukyan dynasty, and the kings of Gujarât were equally zealous in the work.

Bhîmadeva survived the raid of Maḥmûd by nearly thirty years, finally abdicating in 1063, in favour of his son. But these years were not spent in ease; disputes arose

---

[1] Ibn Asir, in Elliot's *Muham. History*, vol. II. p. 471.

with the native chiefs of Râjputânâ and Mâlvâ; and Bhîma in his wars with them, on the whole extended his dominions. He assumed the title of "king of kings," and some of his successors asserted for themselves even more sounding titles. His queen Udayâmatî built the Râṇî's well at Aṇhilavâḍa, of which splendid work only a fragment now remains.

His son Karṇa,—who took the *biruda* or honorific name of Trailokyamalla—ruled for thirty years, till 1093,—a period of national consolidation and great public works,—secular as well as religious. A Jaina temple at Girnâr, the Mudhera tank and temples there, and the great Karṇasâgara—an artificial lake on the Rupen river at Kunsâgar near Mudhera, known from its extent as "the ten miles tank," and of which the embankment broke only in 1814,—are some of the works ascribed to the reign of this king.

To him is also ascribed the foundation of the city of Karṇâvatî on the Sâbarmatî river about 55 miles above where it discharges into the Gulf of Kambhât or Cambay. If tradition may be trusted, the country round where Aḥmadâbâd now stands was then covered with jungle and inhabited by Bhills and allied aboriginal tribes. One of their chiefs named Âshâ of Âshâpalli—now Âshâwal—was defeated and slain by Karṇa, who built temples to Kochrava-devî and Jayantî-devî, and afterwards formed the town of Karṇâvatî or Srî Nagara close by. This afterwards gave rise to the later city of Aḥmadâbâd. Though the temple has long since disappeared, the village of Kochrava is well known close to Aḥmadâbâd on the opposite side of the river, and Âsbâwal is a quarter on the east side of the modern city.

After Karṇadeva's death in 1093 and during the minority of his son Jayasiṁha surnamed Siddharâja, two vast reservoirs surrounded with stone steps—the Mainala Sarovar at Viramgâm and the Malâv or Mainala Talâva at Ḍholkâ—were constructed, and Jaina and Hindu temples built at Karṇâvatî.

Jayasiṁha, the most popular king of the Solankhi race, was also one of the greatest builders, and during his reign of 49 years was largely developed and improved what is sometimes called the Jaina or Gujarât style of architecture in sumptuous edifices and reservoirs. He is said to have restored or rebuilt the great Rudramâlâ shrine at Siddhapur—the largest temple in Western India, the Sahasraliṅga tank at Pâṭan, the Bindosarovar at Siddhapur, the beautiful Sûrya temple at Mudhera, and even the splendid gateways and fortifications of Jhinjhuwâḍâ,[1] with many other similar works. It must be borne in mind, however, that, to a popular and energetic monarch, tradition is only too apt to ascribe works to which he has no historic claim, and this has been pre-eminently the case with Jayasiṁha Siddharâja. The works executed during his long and prosperous reign were many and important, but some of those popularly ascribed to him must belong, as their style indicates, to a period at least a century later.

The capital Aṇhilawâḍâ or Aṇhilapâṭaka under Jayasiṁha and his successor Kumârapâla, during the twelfth century, if not earlier, must have attained to great wealth and splendour, and the state was correspondingly large and prosperous. Al Idrîsî, a contemporary of Jayasiṁha, writing in Sicily, tells his readers that "in all Nahrawâra and its environs, people never travel otherwise than in carriages drawn by bullocks.[2]

---

[1] *The Antiquities of Kâṭhiâwâḍ and Kachh in Arch. Sur. Westn. India*, vol. II. pp. 217, 222.

[2] Abu'l Fazl says "Pâttau produces oxen that will travel fifty kos in half a day."—*Ayin Akbari*, vol. I. p. 65.

These vehicles are furnished with fastenings and straps and serve for the transport of merchandise."

Siddharâja's successor was Kumârapâla who commemorated his rule by many monuments, among which was probably the temple of Somanâtha of which the walls are still standing. During his reign (1143–1173) flourished the famous Jaina scholar Hemâchandra or Hemâchârya who exercised great influence over his sovereign, and, in the later years of his reign at least, seems to have gained him over to his own religion.

The prevalence of the Jainas, and the temples they built from the eleventh century downwards at Abu and elsewhere in Gujarât, has led some to call the Hindu style of Gujarât and the neighbouring Rajputana, the Jaina style, as if it were the style of that sect. The fact, however, is that it is the style of a district and of a period, for the Brahmanical temples of Siddhapur, Somanâtha and Ambarnâtha, are built in the same style as those of the Jainas on Mount Abu and elsewhere; and it is this style adapted to Muhammadan wants that we shall find at a later date characterising the buildings of Aḥmadâbâd, Châmpânir, and other cities of Gujarât. It has affinities with the Chalukyan style of the Dekhan, but is far more closely allied to that which prevailed in the Rajput kingdoms of Central India and Râjputânâ during the tenth and following centuries. Its adaptations to the requirements of the Musalman conquerors of Gujarât in the fourteenth century will be noticed at a later point.

Kumârapâla died at about the age of eighty years in 1173, and was succeeded by his nephew Ajayapâla, a follower of Śaivism—like most of the Solaṅkhi princes; but after three years he was murdered, perhaps through Jaina influence, and was followed first by his young son Mûlarâja II. for about two years, and then by another son (or nephew) Bhîmadeva II., who, during a long reign of sixty-three years (A.D. 1178–1241), had to defend himself as best he could against successive Muhammadan invasions. In the very beginning of his reign, under Muizu'd-dîn bin Sâm, otherwise called Shâhâbu'd-dîn Muhammad Ghori of Gazni, they burst upon Gujarât, but, after a hard fought battle, they were defeated and driven back. Sixteen years later the Sultân's deputy Qutbu'd-dîn Aibak returned to avenge this repulse and plundered Gujarât, but withdrew without effecting the conquest of the country. Wars with the Chauhan of Ajmer had weakened both sovereigns, and though Bhîmadeva and others tried to recover Ajmer from the Muhammadans they were repulsed with terrible loss.

With Tribhuvanapâla the son and successor of Bhîmadeva II., who ruled only for a year or two, the Solankhi or principal branch of the Chaulukya dynasty came to an end in 1244. He was succeeded by Visaladeva, the Vâghelâ or Vyâghrapallî Raṇa of Ḍholkâ, a powerful chief, whose father Vîradhavala had tried to assert his independence since 1220. He was alleged to trace his descent from one Ḍhavala, who had married Kumârapâla's mother's sister,[1] and founded the town of Ḍhavalakkaka or Ḍhavalagṛiha, now Ḍholka. His son was Arṇorâja, whose son Lavaṇaprasîda had perhaps been a minister (*râjyachintâkarî*) under Bhîmadeva. His son Vîradhavala was Bhîmdeva's Yuvarâja or deputy, but died before his father about 1239. This family claimed to be of Chaulukya descent, and Vîsaladeva ruled for eighteen years from 1243, as king of Gujarât. He was a great builder: Dabhoi or Darbhavatî owed its famous Hîra gate

[1] But see *Ind. Ant.*, vol. VI. pp. 197 f. and XI. p. 99.

and temple of Vaidyanâtha to his taste, and many temples were erected at Girnâr, Kambhâyat, Abu, Ḍholka and elsewhere by his great Jaina ministers—the brothers Vastupâla and Tejaḥpâla, and by others during his reign.

Of his son and successor Arjunadeva (1261–1274) and grandson Sârangadeva (1274 to 1296) the records are as yet scanty. The latter was succeeded by his son Karṇa II., surnamed Ghelo or "the insane," in the same year that 'Alâu'd-dîn Khilji basely murdered his uncle and father-in-law the Sulṭân Jalâlu'd-dîn Fîrûz Shâh[1] with the heir Ruknu'd-dîn Ibrâḥim, and seized the throne of Dehlî. Early next year 'Alau'd-dîn sent his wife's brother Sanjar Khân, known as Ulugh Khân, and his prime minister Malik Nasrat Jâlesarî with a large army to Gujarât. They took and plundered Aṇhilavâḍâ, destroying the Rudra Mâla, and ravaged the country as far as Somanâtha which they took, and carried the *Linga* or idol to Dehli "where it was laid down for people to tread upon" as they entered the mosque. At Kambhâyat or Cambay, Nasrat Khân levied from the merchants, who were very wealthy, large quantities of jewels and precious articles; and throughout the country all the finer temples were deliberately wrecked. By repeated expeditions Ulugh Khân completed the subjugation of the country and was appointed *Nâzim* or governor, which office he held for a considerable time, but, at the instigation of his rival Malik Nâib Kafûr Hazâr-dinârî—a slave sent from Kambhâyat by Nasrat Khân—he was recalled by 'Alâu'd-dîn and unjustly put to death in 1315. A serious revolt at once broke out, and Kamâlu'd-dîn Gurg, who was sent by the young Sulṭân Qûtbu'd-dîn Mubârak Shâh to quell it, was slain by the rebel leader and the insurrection spread. Mâlik 'Aînu'l Mulk Multâni was then sent with another army and succeeded in reducing Gujarât again to obedience. Malik Dînâr, the Sulṭân's father-in-law, was then appointed *Wâlî* or governor, with the title of Zafar Khân, and tried to please his superior by sending large sums to the imperial treasury, but after a few months he was recalled by his foolish, violent, and debauched young sovereign and put to death. A base-born upstart, Hisâmu'd-dîn, mother's brother of Hasan Khusrû Khân Parwârî—the favourite slave of the day,—was next sent to Aṇhilawâḍâ, and, immediately collecting his Hindu connexions, he attempted to organise a revolt, but the nobles discovering his design, sent him a prisoner to Dehli, where after giving him a slap on the face the Sulṭân made him one of his personal attendants. Mâlik Wajihu'd-dîn Kuraishî, with the title of Sadaru'l Mulk, next held the governership for a while and restored order, but was afterwards promoted to be Vazîr with the title of Tâju'l-Mulk. Khusrû Khân then procured for himself the appointment of governor of Gujarât, but not content with even this, he assassinated his master, 4th April 1321, and usurped the throne of Dehli as Nasiru'd-dîn Khusrû Shah, only to be murdered in turn, in August following, by Ghâzî Beg Tughlaq,[2] who ascended the throne with the title of Ghiyâsu'd-dîn Tughlaq Shâh I. He appointed Wajihu'd-dîn, who bore the title of Tâju'd-dîn Ja'far, to be Nâzim.

About this time Kambhâyat appears to have been a centre of Muhammadan power, and the large mosque in that city was completed in 1325. On the death of Ghiyâsu'd-dîn in Feb. 1325, his son Muḥammad Tughlaq Shâh (1315–1351) appointed 'Âḥmad Ayyâz as governor who continued till 1338, with Malik Mukbil the son of a musician, who had received the title of Khân Jahân Nâib Bakhtiyâr under him, first as deputy, then as minister, and finally, from about 1338, as governor, which

[1] On the 29th July 1296.

[2] Elliot, *Muham. Hist.*, vol. III. pp. 225 ff.

appointment he held till 1347. This was a time of constant revolts and pillage, the weakness of the government tempted the discontented to plunder. Early in 1345, when near Baroda and Dabhoi with a convoy of treasure and horses for Dehli, Malik Mukbil was attacked by the foreign *Amîrs* who had leagued with the Hindu chiefs, and was utterly routed and plundered. 'Azîz Himar, a depraved royal favourite from Dhâr, who had treacherously put to death about eighty of the foreign *Amîrs* on the mere ground of their being foreigners, and had thus provoked the revolt, immediately marched against the rebels, but was taken and put to an ignominious death. Muḥammad Tughlaq then marched into Gujarât,[1] and with his wonted ferocity suppressed the revolt, sacking Surat and Kambhâyat and putting to death most of the Muhammadan nobles of Bharoch with all other suspected persons. When he left for Devagaḍh to put down another rising there, one Taghî or Taghâ, who had been a cobbler and slave of the general Safdar Mâlik Sulṭânî, raised a fresh rebellion among the Gujarât nobles, seized Paṭṭan, plundered Kambhâyat, laid siege to Bharoch, and put to death Mu'izzu'd-dîn Nizâmu'l-Mulk the governor of Gujarât and other officials.

This led to Muḥammad Shâh's immediate return, and he spent three rainy seasons in Gujarât in putting down the rebels and settling the country. Taghî had fled to Junâgaḍh, and the second wet season (1348) was spent by the Sulṭân there, trying to reduce the Chuḍâsamâ prince[2] of that place. Taghî escaped to Sindh, and Muḥammad, after subduing the coasts and many petty chiefs, spent the next rains at Gondal, where he was taken ill and suffered much from fever. He then crossed over to Sindh in pursuit of Taghî, but died on reaching Ṭhaṭṭâ, 20th March 1351. Shortly before his death he had appointed Amîr Husain bin Mîrân as governor of Gujarât with the titles of Malika'sh-sharq and Nizâmu'l-mulk, but Firuz Shâh on his arrival from Sindh, about 1364, dismissed him because he had not aided the imperial army with provisions on its disastrous march across the desert and Raṇ of Kachh. Zafar Khân, the son-in-law of Sulṭân Fakhru'd-dîn of Sonârgâṅw, was appointed in his stead. The revenues of Gujarât, amounting to twenty million *taṅkas*, were expended on refitting the royal army to return against Ṭhaṭṭâ, and Zafar Khân accompanied it. On his death in 1371, his eldest son Daryâ Khân succeeded to his fief, but seems to have lived mostly at court and ruled Gujarât by a deputy named Malik Zîâu'l-mulk Malik Shamsu'd-dîn Abûrjâ. Shamsu'd-dîn Dâmaghânî having offered to the Sulṭân to increase the usual revenue by four million *taṅkas*, 100 elephants, 200 Arab horses, and 400 slaves—children of Hindu chiefs and Abyssinians,—an offer was first made to Daryâ Khân to confirm him in the government if he would make this offer. Knowing who had made so extravagant a promise, he declined,[3] and Shamsu'd-dîn was put in his place. He quickly raised a rebellion in the province, and was slain and his head sent to Dehli in 1377.[4]

The next governor was Malik Mufarrih Sulṭânî with the title of Farhatu'l-mulk Rasti Khân, and on the assumption of sovereignty by Nâsiru'd-dîn Muḥammad Shâh

[1] Conf. Elliot, *Hist. Ind.*, vol. III. p. 260.

[2] The Muhammadan historians call him Khaṅgâr, but Khaṅgâr IV.—if we may trust the *Târikh i-Sorath*—died in 1333 ; and the prince now on the throne was perhaps Mokalasiṁha or Mugatsiṁha, 1345 to 1359.

[3] He was put to death by Jaunân Shâh Khân-i-Jahân in 1387.

[4] Elliot, *Muham. Hist.*, vol. III. p. 324 ; Briggs's *Firishtah*, vol. I. p. 455.

Tughlaq II. in 1387, Malik Ya'kûb Muḥammad Hâji, master of the horse, was styled Sikandar Khân and sent to supersede Malik Mufarrih. On arriving in Gujarât, however, the latter, at the head of the nobles, rose against him and slew him.

During the troubles that immediately followed no change was made, but in 1391, on the occasion of a second revolt of Farhatu'l-Mulk, Zafar or Muẓaffar Khân, son of Wajîhu'l-Mulk, was sent against him, and in an engagement at Jitpur near Kambha, a dependency of Pâṭṭan, Farhat was defeated and slain 4th January 1392. This Zafar Khân's father is said to have been a Hindu of the Tâṅka tribe of Rajputs,[1] a chief of Thâsrâ in the Kheḍâ district of Gujarât and named Sadhâran, who was converted to Islâm and took the name of Wajihu'l-Mulk, while his brother Sadhu was re-named Shamsher Khân. Muẓaffar Khân extended the Muhammadan power in Gujarât; exacted tribute from the chief of Junâgaḍh (1395); invaded Mâlwâ and after various successes returned to Nahrawâlâ in 1396; destroyed the temple of Somanâtha; marched against the chief of Idar, and probably built the mosque there. Finally, favoured by the invasion of the Mughals under Saheb Kirân Amîr Tîmûr Gûrgan, commonly known as Timurlang in 1398, Muẓaffar assumed the position of an independent prince.

This hurried résumé of a century's history of Gujarât may suffice to show how little calculated the Musulmân rule then was to foster any art or handicraft. It was a period of rapine and plunder and almost certainly of untold suffering. Yet we are not without monuments of this time. The great mosque at Bharoch, however, shows how they were erected: the Hindu and Jaina temples were torn down and their materials re-arranged to suit the wants of the destroyers.

In 1403, Muẓaffar's son Tâtâr Khân is said to have seized his father and sent him prisoner to Asâwal. Tâtâr then assumed the titles of royalty under the style of Sulṭân Nasîru'd-dîn Muhammad Shâh, and collected an army to march against Dehli but was poisoned at Paṭṭan by Shams Khân. His father was brought from Asâwal by night and the whole army at once submitted to him (1404). At the request of the nobles he assumed royal honours as Muẓaffar Shâh. He then took Dhâr and consolidated his power, but after an expedition, perhaps against Kachh, he died in July 1410 in the seventieth year of his age, not altogether without suspicions of having been poisoned by his grandson Aḥmad whom he had already employed in a warlike expedition into Mâlwâ.

After some struggles with his relatives and others, Aḥmad Shâh got securely established on the throne of Gujarât and reduced many hitherto almost independent districts, forcing on the inhabitants the Muslim religion.

In the first year of his reign (1410–11) he founded the city of Aḥmadâbâd on the left bank of the Sâbarmatî river, near the old town of Asâwal and probably on the site of Karṇâvatî, founded by Karṇadeva I. The fort, he erected round the site of an old temple of Bhadrakâli—the terrific and bloody form of Durgâ;—and from this the fort still retains the name of "the Bhadr." As a strict Muhammadan he erected a mosque within it, constructed from the materials of the Hindu temples.

[1] Regarding the Tâṅka tribe, see Beames's ed. of Elliot's *Races of the N.W. Provs.*, vol. I. pp. 109, 114; Tod's *Râjasthân*, vol. I. pp. 103 ff. (Madras ed. pp. 94 ff.).

While his new capital was being built, Aḥmad Shâh was busy destroying the temples of the Hindûs, forcing their chiefs to embrace Islâm, carrying off their daughters, and consolidating his power. In 1415, he destroyed the temple at Siddhapur; in 1416, he marched against Dhâr; and in 1419 he ravaged the lands round Soṅgaḍh on the Khandesh frontier and built a fort with a mosque there. Next year he built the fort of Dohad on the Mâlwâ border; and in 1427, that of Aḥmadnagar, as a check on the râv of Îdar. In 1431, he attacked Thâṇâ, near Bombay, and took it. He was in fact almost continually engaged in war, and pressed his conquests as far as Koṭâ and Bundî. In 1442[1] he died, after a reign of thirty-two years.

Under Aḥmad Shâh's successors Aḥmadâbâd steadily rose to be the finest city in India. "The situation," says Abul Fazl,[2] writing towards the end of the sixteenth century, "is remarkably healthy, and you may here provide yourself with the productions of every part of the globe. There are two forts, on the outside of which is the town, which formerly consisted of three hundred and sixty puras (or quarters) but now (in 1590) only eighty-four are in a flourishing condition. In these are a thousand stone masjids, each having two large minarets and many wonderful inscriptions." Each mohalla or quarter, as Firishtah tells us,[3] had a wall surrounding it; the principal streets were sufficiently wide to admit of ten carriages abreast; and "it is hardly necessary to add," he says, "that this is, on the whole, the handsomest city in Hindustan and perhaps in the world."

'Aḥmad Shâh was succeeded by his son Muhammad Shâh Karîm Ghiyâsu'd-dunya wa-u'd-dîn, styled Zerbakhsh or "Gold-bestower." Marching upon Châmpânir, the native chief called in the aid of Mâḥmud Khilji of Mâlwâ, when Muḥammad Shâh prepared for flight. The nobles caused him to be poisoned and set up his son Jalâl Khân as Quṭbu'd-dîn Shâh 12th February 1451. Mâhmud Khilji now took Sulṭânpur, and marched into the Bharoch district and then by Naḍiâd to Baroda, which he plundered but was defeated by Quṭbu'd-dîn at Kâpadvaṅj after a sometime doubtful struggle, 1454. Quṭbu'd-dîn next interfered on behalf of the Nâgor chief against the Râṇâ of Chittor, deprived the latter of Mount Abu which he bestowed on the Devra chief of Sirohi. He then besieged Chittor, but on the Râṇâ promising to pay tribute he did not press the siege.

Quṭbu'd-dîn died 24 May 1459 and was buried in the vault of his father Muḥammad Shâh. In his reign the buildings erected at Ahmadâbâd and still remaining are the mosques of Quṭbu'd-dîn and Malik Shâbân, the Kankâriya lake, the tomb of Shâh Aḥmad Khaṭṭû at Sarkhej, the small shrine at Batwâ, and Daryâ Khân's tomb.

His uncle Daud was raised to the throne but soon deposed because of his follies. Faṭh Khân, son of Muḥammad Shâh and grandson of Aḥmad Shâh by Bîbî Moghlâi, a youth of fourteen, was now elected (June 1459), with the title of Shamsu'l-Mulûk wa'l-ḥaq Nâṣiru'd-dunyâ wa'd-dîn Abu'l Faṭh Maḥmud. He is usually styled Bîgarah or Baiqara, and was perhaps the greatest of the Gujarât kings. Twice he delivered Nizâm Shâh, the Bahmani sovereign, from the attacks of Maḥmud Khilji. In 1467

[1] The *Tabaqat Akbari* says on the 4th Rabî'ul âkhar 846; the *Tarikh-i Alfi* also gives 846; Briggs's *Firishtah* has 4th Rabî'ul avval 847 or July 4th, 1443.

[2] Gladwin's *Ayeen Akbari*, vol. II. p. 63.

[3] Briggs's *Firishtah*, vol. IV. p. 14.

he attacked Râo Maṇḍalik of Junâgaḍh, and, after repeated invasions, reduced Soraṭh to a province in 1472, governed by officers appointed by the king. At Junâgaḍh, he erected the large mosque[1] and a palace, and renamed the town Mustafâbâd. During his absence from Aḥmadâbâd, Malik Jamâlu'd-dîn was governor of the city with the title of Muḥâfiẓ Khân, the same who afterwards built the very beautiful private mosque that still goes by his name. Maḥmûd next invaded Kachh[2] and completely defeated the Sumrâ and Sodhâ chiefs, then he turned his arms against the pirates of Dwârka or Jagat, whom he defeated with great slaughter, took the fort, sent Bhîmarâja prisoner to Aḥmadâbâd to be hewn in pieces there, and destroyed the idol temples, building a mosque in their place. On his return he equipped a fleet at Goghâ to chastise the pirates of the Malabar coast, and then went back to Aḥmadâbâd by way of Kambhâyat. In 1479 he sent an army to ravage the country round Châmpânir, and about the same time he founded the city of Maḥmûdâbâd on the Wâtrak river about eighteen miles south of Aḥmadâbâd. In 1482 the Râwal of Châmpânir having killed one of Maḥmûd's officers who was making forays into his territory, war was declared against him. Sultân Ghiyâsu'd-dîn Khilji of Mâlwâ advanced to aid the Râwal, but Maḥmûd marched to Dohad to meet him and he retired. After a long siege, Châmpânir was taken in 1484 and the remains of the garrison put to the sword. Maḥmûd now built a wall round the town of Châmpânir at the foot of Pâwâgaḍh hill and named the place Muḥammadâbâd, which speedily rose to be a large and rich city. All that now remains of it, however, is portions of the wall, the fine large Jâmî' Masjid and other mosques and tombs built at this period, and now hidden away among trees and thick undergrowth.

After this, in 1487, he caused Aḥmadâbâd to be surrounded by a wall and bastions, and in commemoration of the date of their completion he caused to be inscribed on the face of the fortification the sentence—

من دخله كان امنا

i.e., "Whoever is within is safe";—the numerical values of the letters making 892, the Hijra date.

He planted the streets of the city with trees, adorned it and its suburbs with splendid buildings, and carefully fostered its trade and handicrafts. Among the buildings still left, belonging to this reign, are the Sârangpur Queen's mosque, Dastur Khân's, Muḥâfiẓ Khân's, Miyan Khân Chishti's, Achut Bîbî's, and Sayyad Usman's mosques, parts of the Shâh 'Alam and Batwâ buildings, and Dâdâ Harir's step-well and mosque. Aḥmadâbâd at this period had attained to great wealth, size, and splendour; and though Châmpânir was a favourite residence of the king, and must have been largely peopled from the older capital, it did not diminish its importance. It had good streets, squares, and houses of stone and whitewashed brick with flat roofs.[3]

In 1506, the Gujarât squadron combined with the Turkish fleet and defeated the Portuguese off Chaul; and in 1508 Maḥmûd was able to secure for his nephew Mîrân Muḥammad 'Adil Khân Fârukhi the throne of Khandesh. Maḥmûd died 22 Nov. 1511,

---

[1] *Arch. Sur. West. Ind.*, vol. II. p. 144 and pl. xxv.

[2] The Kachh annals are deficient in dates, but this was probably in the time of Jâm Kânyoji, whose capital was at Ajâpur.

[3] Stanley's *Barbosa*, p. 58.

in the seventieth year of his age, and was buried at Sarkhej in the mausoleum of Shaikh Aḥmad Khaṭṭû.

For the next half century or more, under his successors, Aḥmadâbâd considerably declined, and never afterwards recovered its former greatness. Sulṭân Maḥmûd Shâh I. was succeeded by his son Khalil Khân, whose mother was Râṇî Hîrabâî the daughter of a Râjput chieftain, Râṇâ Nâkha, who lived on the banks of the Mahî. He was forty-one years of age and assumed the title of Muẓaffar Shâh II. Medani Râi, the Hindu minister of Maḥmûd Khilji of Mâlwâ, attempting to dethrone his master and being aided by the Râṇâ of Chittor, Muẓaffar had to contend with both, and having captured Mându in 1518, he reinstated Maḥmûd. The Chittor Râna, Sangram, however, again invaded Mâlwâ and even Gujarât and had a second time to be resisted. During this reign the kingdom was prosperous and cultivation was greatly extended, especially in Jhâlâwâd. Muẓaffar died 17th February 1526.

He was succeeded by his son Sikandar Shâh, who, after a reign of about three and a half months, was assassinated by Imadu'l-mulk Khush Kadam on 30th May, when his younger brother Nâṣir Khân was raised to the throne with the title of Maḥmûd Shâh II. He reigned about three months, when an older brother Bahâdur Shâh, returning from Jaunpur, deprived him of the kingdom, captured and executed Imadu'l-Mulk, and mounted the throne, 20th August 1526. His brother Latif Khân sought to deprive him of his rule, but was defeated and died of his wounds. Bahâdur directed the construction of the fortress of Bharoch, and was almost constantly engaged in war. The Portuguese, who wanted possession of Diu, had to be watched and frustrated. He twice invaded the Dekhan in aid of the Khandesh and Berar rulers against Burhân Nizâm Shâh of Aḥmadnagar; he subdued Mâlwâ in 1531; annexed Vîramgâm and Mândal in Jhâlâwaḍ, and Raisin, Bhilsâ and Chanderi in Mâlwâ; attacked Chittor but was bought off; and captured Ranthambor. Having offended Humâyûn of Dehli, however, the Mughal sulṭân attacked him just after he had captured Chittor in 1535 and defeated his army. Humâyûn, following up his first success, took Mându and then Châmpânir and finally all Gujarât except the peninsula. Fortunately for Bahâdur at this juncture Sher Shâh revolted in Bihâr and Jaunpur, and Humâyûn had to proceed to the north, leaving his brother Hindâl Mîrzâ, his uncle Mîrzâ Yâdgâr Nâsir, and other officers in charge of Gujarât. The Gujarât nobles[1] at once rose against the Mughals, and, with Bahâdur at their head, they defeated Mîrzâ 'Askarî and the imperial armies near Maḥmûdâbâd and expelled them from the country in 1536. Meantime, Bahâdur having had to court the aid of the Portuguese had granted them permission to build a factory at Diu, which they fortified. Repenting of his action he wished to expel them, but was inveigled into visiting the viceroy on board his ship, and while returning in his barge was barbarously slain, 14th February 1537, in the 31st year of his age.

During the next thirty-seven years, Gujarât was torn by factions, the chief nobles in turn setting up minors as puppet kings. The first of these was Mîrân Muḥammad Shâh II. Âsiri, the nephew of Bahâdur Shâh, who died shortly after his accession.

---

[1] Ghazanfar Kokah, brother of Mahdî Qâsim Khân, was imprisoned by Mîrzâ 'Askarî the governor of Aḥmadâbâd, but escaped to Diu and betrayed to Sulṭân Bahâdur the schemes of 'Askarî.—Blochmann's *Ain-i Akbari*, vol. I. p. 348.

The nobles then crowned Muḥammad Khân, son of Latif Khan the brother of Bahâdur, a boy of eleven years,—Daryâ Khân and Imâdu'l-Mulk ruling in his name. The former, however, soon expelled Imâdu'l-Mulk, but let Âlam Khân Lodhi manage affairs, and he revolting, with the king's aid, finally overthrew Daryâ Khân, but was in turn driven out. About 1545 this Muḥammad III. began to resume the lands granted to Rajput chiefs on his north-eastern frontier and to persecute the Hindûs, thus provoking disturbances. Quarrels also rose among the nobles, owing to the king's partiality for low-born favourites; and in 1554 he was murdered by Burhân, one of his own servants.

The nobles, with I'tmâd Khân the prime minister, now set up Qaziu'l-Mulk with the title of Aḥmad Shâh II. (15th February 1554), pretending that he was the son of Prince Aḥmad Khân formerly governor of Ahmadâbâd; but—after a troubled reign of seven years, during which the intrigues and quarrels of the nobles weakened the state and left the king no real influence—he was found murdered at the foot of the palace wall, April 21st, 1561.

I'tmâd Khân, the prime minister who had caused the murder of Aḥmad Shâh II., now set up a youth named Nathû, whom he styled Muẓaffar Shâh III., alleging that he was a posthumous son of Maḥmûd Shâh. I'tmâd Khân, however, provoked the other nobles by his assumptions, and the country was parcelled out among the Amîrs and continued in a state of civil war. In 1571 the Mirzâs sons of Husain of Khorâsân having quarrelled with Akbar came to Gujarât and joined Changiz Khân, son of I'tmâdu'l Mulk, a Turkish slave and one of the most powerful opponents of I'tmâd Khân, who now marched on Aḥmadâbâd and within eight miles of the city defeated I'tmâd Khân Gujarâtî and Sayyâd Mîrân bin Mubârâk, taking possession of the capital. I'tmâd Khân fled with the king to Morâsâ, and after some further attempts to regain his power he invited the emperor Akbar, who was only too glad of a pretext for driving out the Mirzâs and reducing Gujarât under his own imperial sway. He accordingly marched on Aḥmadâbâd, which he took possession of on 20th November 1572, and thus put an end to the separate kingdom of Gujarât. Muẓaffar Shâh, who had abdicated in favour of Akbar, was sent to Agra, and subsequently placed in close confinement.

Gujarât was now again governed by viceroys appointed by the court of Dehli. Akbar's first governor was his foster brother Khân-i A'zam called Mîrzâ Azîz Kokâ or Kokaltâsh, while to other nobles provincial commands were assigned. But no sooner had Akbar himself retired than the old Gujarât nobles, together with the Mîrzâ Muḥammad Husain, attacked the new rulers with such success that Akbar had to make forced marches to their relief, and,—defeating the rebels before Aḥmadâbâd,—after only eleven days' stay, returned to Agra. Mîrzâ 'Aziz Kokâ in 1575 retired into private life and 'Abdu'r-Rahîm Khân, surnamed Khân Mîrzâ,[1] son of Bairâm Khân, and only about nineteen years of age, was made viceroy, but under the guidance of his deputy Wazîr Khân.. The administration, however, was unsatisfactory and Râja Todar Mal was sent to make a revenue settlement of the province, while Wajihu'l Mulk Gujarâti was appointed *diwân* to administer civil justice under the viceroy.

---

[1] Blochmann's *Ain-i Akbari*, vol. I. p. 334.

In the latter part of 1577, Shahâbu'd-dîn Aḥmad Khân was appointed viceroy, and began to strengthen his military posts and to settle the revenue, when his nephew Mîrzâ Khân—sent against Amin Khân Ghori, who had continued to hold Junagaḍh—was totally defeated by that chief and his ally the Jâm of Nâwanagar, while at the same time Muẓaffar Shâh III. having escaped from his confinement in 1578, arrived in Gujarât, and collecting a respectable army was joined by 700 or 800 Mughals at Khiri in Sardhâr. I'tmâd Khân Gujarâti, again restored to favour, had just been appointed viceroy, when Muẓaffar Shâh took Aḥmadâbâd in 1583, and then meeting I'tmâd Khan and Shahâbu'd-dîn, who had returned to assist, he inflicted a severe defeat on them. Quṭbu'd-dîn Muḥammad Khân, one of the imperial commanders,[1] now advanced from the Khandesh frontier by forced marches and threw himself into Baroda, where he was besieged by Muẓaffar, and being induced by promises to come out to treat for peace, he was treacherously killed. Bharoch was also surrendered to Muẓaffar, who was now reinstated king of Gujarât.

At the close of 1583 Akbar, a second time, sent Mîrzâ Khân to Gujarât as viceroy. Muẓaffar hastening from Bharoch met him at Sarkhej near Aḥmadâbâd, where a pitched battle was fought 22nd January 1584, in which Muẓaffar was entirely defeated and fled to Kambhât; he was again defeated by Mirzâ Khân at Nadol, and thence he escaped to Râjpiplâ. For these two victories Akbar bestowed the rank of Khânkhânân on the viceroy. Muẓaffar fled to Gondal, and after being cheated by Amîn Khân Ghorî of Junâgaḍh out of two lakhs of *Mahmudîs*,[2] by promises of aid, he was left to be hunted by the viceroy in the Baradâ hills. Thence he escaped, and after another defeat in Gujarât, again found refuge in Râjpiplâ.

In 1590 the Khânkhânân, who had laboured for the prosperity of the country, was recalled and Ismâ'il Qulî Khân appointed viceroy; but in a few months he was superseded by Mîrzâ 'Azîz Kokaltâsh, for the second time governor. Muẓaffar again returned to Soraṭh in 1591 and was joined by the chiefs of Nâwânagar and Kachh[3] and Daulat Khân Ghori of Junâgadh. The viceroy marched into the peninsula with a powerful army, defeated Muẓaffar and the Jâm; took and plundered Nâwânagar; and laid siege to Junâgaḍh, where Muẓaffar and the Jâm had fled for refuge; but he had to retire for want of grain. After seven or eight months the viceroy again marched against Junâgaḍh and, binding the Jâm to provide supplies of grain, after a siege of three months, the garrison surrendered. Muẓaffar had now taken refuge at Dwârkâ and on being pursued he escaped to Kachh, where the chief delivered him up to a force sent to secure him. On the way to the viceroy's camp at Morbi, Muẓaffar cut his throat with a razor, and his head was then cut off and sent to the imperial court by the viceroy. A'zam Khân was now summoned to court 1592, but his friends representing to him that Akbar was displeased with him and was seeking an opportunity to imprison him, without leave or notice he set sail with his family for Makka 13th March 1594, O.S.[4]

---

1 He belonged to the Atgah Khail and founded several mosques, &c. at Lahor.

2 The *Mahmudî* and *Changizi* were about equal, but varied in value from about 7½ to 11 annas, that is from 19 to 28 *dams* or from 47 to 79 *tankhâs*. At the rate of 20 *dams* or 50 *tankhâs* to the *Mahmudî*, the sum obtained from Muzaffer by Amin Khân would be equal to about 1,00,000 rupees.

3 Râo Bhârmal (A.D. 1585–1631) son of Khangâr.

4 The Hijra date given by other writers is 1st Rajab 1002. He returned to Virâwal in the beginning of 1003, and was made governor of Bihâr.

In 1595 Sulṭân Murâd Mîrzâ second son of Akbar was sent as viceroy, but going soon after to the Dekhan, Surajsingh was appointed deputy in Gujarât and defeated Bahâdur, son of the late Muẓaffar Shâh, who had excited a rebellion. Murâd Mîrzâ having died 1st May 1599, Mirzâ 'Aziz was appointed for the third time, and sent Shamsu'd-dîn Husain as his deputy to Ahmadâbâd. In 1602 he made his eldest son Shâdmân his deputy; and on the accession of Jahângir, Oct. 16th, 1605, Qulij Khân was appointed to Gujarât, but he did not join the appointment, allowing Azîz Kokâ to act till the latter was transferred to Lahor in 1606. Then Sayyid Shaikh Farid Murtazâ Khân-i Bukhârî was put in charge of the province. Almost his only act was to repair the fort of Kaḍi about 27 miles north-west from Aḥmadâbâd. His relatives oppressed the people and disturbances broke out among the native chiefs and forces had to be sent from the north to suppress them. In 1609 Mîrzâ 'Aziz Koka was again made viceroy but remained at court sending his son Jahângîr Qulî Khân as his deputy, and after two years was succeeded by 'Abdullah Khân Bahâdur Firûz-Jang as 13th viceroy, with Ghiyâsu'd-dîn as his minister, and with orders to avenge a recent inroad by Malik 'Ambar Habshi governor of Daulatâbâd. This was unsuccessful, and in 1616 he was sent a second time with the prince Shâh-Jahân, when Malik 'Ambar gave up most of the places taken from the Mughals, and most of the other Dekhan princes submitted. On his return to Dehli, Shaikh Hassû Muqarrab Khân was appointed to the government, with Muḥammad Safi as his *diwân* but he gave no satisfaction and was recalled. Jahângir visited Gujarat in person and hunted elephants in the Dohad and Châmpânir forests, but did not enjoy the climate of Ahmadâbâd.[1]

The successive viceroys after this were as follows:—

Prince Khurram, afterwards Shâh Jahân who built the Shâhi Bâgh, 1616.[2]

Sulṭân Dâwar Bakhsh surnamed Mirzâ Bulâqî, son of Sultân Khusro, 1622, with Khân 'Azim Mîrzâ Azîz Kokaltâsh as adviser.[3]

Khân Jahân deputy viceroy, sent by Shâh Jahân to the emperor, and Muḥammad Safi, styled Saif Khân acted, with Yusuf Khân as minister, 1624.

Sher Khân Tar, with Khwâjah Haiyât as minister, 1627.

Islâm Khân, with Khwâjah Jahân as minister, 1632.

Bâqir Khân, Riâyat Khân being minister, 1632.

Sipahdâr Khân, foster-brother of Aurangzib,—Riâyat Khân continuing as minister, 1633.

Saif Khân, 1635.

Mîr Muhammad Bâqir with the title of 'Azam Khân,[4] end of 1635, with Riâyat Khân and afterwards Mîr Muḥammad Sâbar as ministers. In his time the viceroyal residence (now used as the Jail) was built. It was during his governorship that the

---

[1] Jahângir disliked Ahmadâbâd and abused it heartily.—Elliot's *Muham. Hist.* vol. VI. p. 358; conf. Douglas's *Bombay and Westn. India*, vol. I. pp. 301.

[2] Sir Thomas Roe's *Journal*, ch. ix.

[3] This noble, so often in authority in Gujarât, died at Ahmadâbâd in 1624, and was buried close to his father in 'Azim Khan's mausoleum at Dehli, where a splendid marble monument was erected over his tomb,—called *Chaunsa'th Kambh* from its sixty-four pillars.

[4] He was the brother of 'Asaf Khân Ja'far Beg, who held the post of *Wazarat* under Jahângir. They were natives of Qazwin in Persia. 'Azam Khân, born 1575, was at different times governor of Bengal, Allahâbâd, Gujarât, and Jaunpur—at the last of which he died, 1649. Conf. *Voy. de Olearius* (Paris, 1659) tom. II. pp. 148, 150.

Sieur de Mandelslo visited Gujurât, and while he gives a glowing picture of the pomp and wealth of 'Azam Khân, he testifies to the oppression by which it was supported and the coarse cruelty of the governor.[1]

Mîrzâ 'Isa Tarkhân, 1642, with Muizu'l Mulk as minister.

Prince Muhammad Aurangzib, 1644, with the same minister.

Shaishta Khân,[2] 1647 ; and in 1648, Hâfiz Muhammad Nâsir as minister.

Prince Muḥammad Dârah Shikoh, and in 1651, Mîr Yahya as minister.

Shaista Khân, a second time, 1652.

Prince Muḥammad Murâd Bakhsh, 1654, with Diânat Khân, and then Rahmat Khân as ministers.

Qâsim Khân, 1657.

Shâh Nawâẓ Khân Safâvi, father-in-law of Aurangzib, 1659.

Jaswantsingh of Jodhpur, 1659.

Mahâbat Khân, 1662. In his time Jean de Thevenot (1633–1667) visited Ahmadâbâd, which he describes as a league and a half in length, including the suburbs, which must have extended a good way to the south and south-east.

Bahâdur Khân Khân Jahân, 1668.

Jaswantsingh, a second time, 1671.

Muḥammad Amin Khân Umdatu'l Mulk, 1674.

Muḥammad Amin Khân, son of Muḥammad Sayyîd Mîr Jumla, 1678,—died at Ahmadâbâd, 15th May 1682.

Mukhtar Khân, 1683.

Prince Muhammad 'Azam Shâh, 1686 ; but immediately after Kârtalab Khân.

Prince Muhammad, son of Aurangzib, a second time, 1703.

Ibrâhim Khân, 1705,—'Abdu'l Hamid Khân acting till his arrival ; the Marâṭhas attacked and defeated the Musalmans at Ratanpur, and again at Bâhâ Piyârâ ford on the Narmadâ, and then retired.

Prince Muḥammad Bedâr Bakht, 1705, during whose time the country was much disturbed. Ibrahim Khân was then ordered to join his government, which he did in 1706.

Immediately after Aurangzib's death in 1707 the Marâṭhas under Bâlâji Viśvanâth invaded the province by way of Jhâbuâ and Godhrâ, where they were ineffectually opposed by Morâd Bakhsh, and advanced by Mundâ and Naḍiâd towards Aḥmadâbâd, but were bought off by a tribute of Rs. 2,10,000, and withdrew. On prince Muḥammad Mu'azzam Shâh acquiring the throne of Dehli as Bahâdur Shah in June 1707, Ibrâhim Khân went to Dehli and resigned his office.

Ghâziu'd-dîn Khân Bahâdur Firuz Jang was appointed to succeed Ibrâhim Khân in 1708 ; and in 1709 Shariat Khân, brother of 'Abdu'l Hamid Khân, was appointed minister in place of his brother who was made chief Qâzi. This viceroy died in 1710. Amânat Khân, governor of Surat, was appointed deputy viceroy in 1711 with the title of Shahâmat Khân. The Marâṭhas again invaded Gujarât when Shahâmat Khân

---

[1] *Voyage*, tom. II. pp. 147 ff.

[2] The builder of a large mosque on the banks of the Jamna, to the west of Allahâbâd fort, completed in A.H. 1056 (A.D. 1646) and destroyed in 1857. By his injustice while governor of Bengal, he provoked a war with Job Charnock. He died in 1694.

ordered Sayyid Aḥmad Gilâni governor of Soraṭh to aid him, and meeting the Marâṭhas at Aṅkleśvar he defeated them.

On the death of the emperor in 1712 Âsafu'd-daula Asad Khân Bahâdur was appointed viceroy by his son Abu'l Faṭh Maghru'd-dîn Jahândâr Shâh, the new Sulṭân, with Muḥammad Khân Beg as deputy.

Shahâmat Khân was appointed viceroy in 1713, but early in 1714, he was superseded by—

Daud Khân Panni, in whose time many of the Hindu bankers of Aḥmadâbâd were plundered by the Musalmans.

In 1715 Mahârâja Ajitsingh of Mârwâr was appointed viceroy, and his son Abhayasingh governor of Soraṭh.

In 1716 Samsâmu'd-daula Basârat Jang Bahâdur was the next viceroy, with Haidar Quli Khân as deputy.

In 1719 Mahârâja Ajitsingh was again made viceroy by the Sayyids who had set up the latest sulṭâns at Dehlî. Pilaji Gaikwâḍ now invaded Gujarât and defeated the imperial troops, and soon after established himself at Songaḍh. The imperial power was now doomed. In 1720 Ajitsingh sent Anupsingh Bhandâri as his deputy to Gujarât.

In 1721 Haidar Quli Khân,—who together with Muḥammad Âmin and Sâ'adat Khân had freed the emperor from the power of the Sayyids,—was appointed viceroy with the title of Muizu'd-daulah Haidar Quli Khân Bahâdur Zafir Jang, and Mâsum Quli Khân received the title of Sujâ'at Khân Bahâdur and the post of deputy viceroy. The people of Aḥmadâbâd immediately attacked the palace of the vile Anupsingh in the Bhadr and he escaped with difficulty. Shujâ'at Khân attacked the house of Nahar Khân who had been Ajitsingh's minister, but on his paying a lakh of rupees he was permitted to leave the city. Shujâ'at Khân next interfered with the Bâbis,—obliged Muhammad Khân Bâbi, governor of Kheḍa, to pay him Rs. 10,000; Qâsam 'Âli Khân, one of the viceroy's officers having been killed at Piṭhâpur, he burnt the town; after exacting tribute in Soraṭh, he passed into Kachh, defeated the chief, and agreed to receive a tribute of 675,000 *mahmudis*—about three and a quarter lakhs of rupees. In 1722 Haidar Quli Khân took up the viceroyalty in person, but, showing signs of independence, he was quickly recalled.

Jumlatu'l Muluk Nizâmu'l Mulk was appointed to succeed Haidar Quli Khân, and directed Safdar Khân Bâbi to act as his deputy and Hâmid Khân as minister with Momin Khân as governor of Surat. Pilâji Gaikwâḍ defeated Momin Khân in 1723 and levied contributions on, and overran the country round Surat; Kântâji Kadam Bânde also invaded the province on the Dohad side. This was the first time the Maraṭhas imposed a regular tribute in Gujarât.

Mubârizu'l Mulk Sarbuland Khân Bahâdur Dilâwar Jang was in 1723 appointed viceroy in place of the Nizâm who had, without leave, gone to the Dekhan. He made Sujâ'at Khân his deputy. He was at first opposed by Hâmid Khân the uncle and deputy of the Nizâm, but the latter was obliged to withdraw to Dohad whence, in concert with Kantâji Kadam Bânde, at the instigation of the Nizâm, he marched on Aḥmadâbâd, defeated Shujâ'at Khân at Mota Medrâ six miles from the city, and slew him, 1724. The Marâthâs now proceeded to collect their one fourth (*chauth*) and one tenth (*sardeshmukhi*) shares of the revenue. Hâmid Khân was practically independent but being opposed by Rustam 'Ali Khân, governor of Surat, both parties engaged the aid of the Marâṭhas, and in the battle of Arâs, Hâmid Khân was defeated and the treacherous Marâṭhas on each side plundered the camps of their allies. They afterwards attacked and defeated Rustam 'Ali, and made an arrangement with Hâmid Khân. Mubârizu'l Mulk was then sent from Dehli with a strong force against both Hâmid Khân and the Marâṭhas, 1725. War continued and the country was plundered by all parties—the Peshwâ contending with Pilâji Gaikwâḍ for the Marâṭha influence in the country.

Abhayasiṁha Mahârâja of Jodhpur was appointed 54th viceroy in 1730, but was opposed and twice defeated by Mubârizu'l-Mulk and had to purchase the surrender by him of Aḥmadâbâd. Abhayasiṁha effected the assassination of Pilâji Gaikwâḍ at Dakor, and then recovered Baroda in 1732, and going to court the following year, left Ratnasingh Bhandâri as deputy viceroy. Rivalries and contests still harassed and desolated the country.

In 1737 Momin Khân was appointed fifty-fifth viceroy with the title of Najmu'd-daulah Momin Khân Firuz Jang, and was quickly forced to ally himself with the Marâṭhas against the supporters of his predecessor, who was ostensibly re-appointed viceroy, while Momin Khân was secretly instructed to oppose him. On his partial success he was again appointed viceroy in 1738, and the contests were continued between him and the Marâṭhas till his death in 1743. After a time his son Muftâkhir Khân was appointed viceroy with the title of Momin Khân but was powerless to act against his rivals. The following year Fakhru'd-daulah Fakhru'd-dîn Khân Shujâ'at Jang Bahâdur was installed in his room, and in 1748 Mahârâja Vakhatsingh, brother of Abhayasing was appointed, but never took up the appointment. Taking advantage of the absence of the governor in the north, Raghunâthrâv joined Dâmâji Gaikwâḍ and marched on Aḥmadâbâd, 1753, but Jawân Mard Khân, hearing of this, returned by forced marches and energetically defended the city : finally a treaty was arranged and the city given up : the suburbs were not repopulated, disorders increased, and the population was oppressed by the Marâṭhas, who also seized on the mosques and destroyed many of them for the materials with which to erect other buildings. In 1755 the rains were very heavy and many parts of the city walls fell down. Momin Khân learning of this marched from Kambhât and retook the city. The Peshwâ and Gaikwâḍ combined to retake it and after a long siege Momin Khân capitulated, April, 1757. In 1760 the Marâṭha power was finally established in Gujarât ; the Gaikwâḍ and Peshwâ divided the revenues.

In 1780 a British force under General Goddard acting in aid of Faṭh Sing Gaikwâḍ against the Peshwâ took Aḥmadâbâd by storm. It was restored to the Peshwâ in 1783, but from about 1799 till 1814 the revenues were farmed by the Gaikwâḍ. Then it was resumed by the Peshwâ and his officers, anxious to collect money, extorted it by every process of oppression[1] for about three years. In 1817 it was ceded to the Gaikwâḍ on an annual rental of four and a half lakhs of rupees, and shortly after it was arranged to hand it over to the British, partly in lieu of payment of a subsidiary force and partly for an exchange of territory near Baroda.

[1] Hamilton, *Desc. of Hindustan*, vol. I. pp. 697, 698.

PLATE II.

H. COUSENS, PHOTO.

BHAROCH: INTERIOR OF THE JAMI MASJID.

PLATE III.

BHAROCH: PLAN OF THE JAMI MASJID.

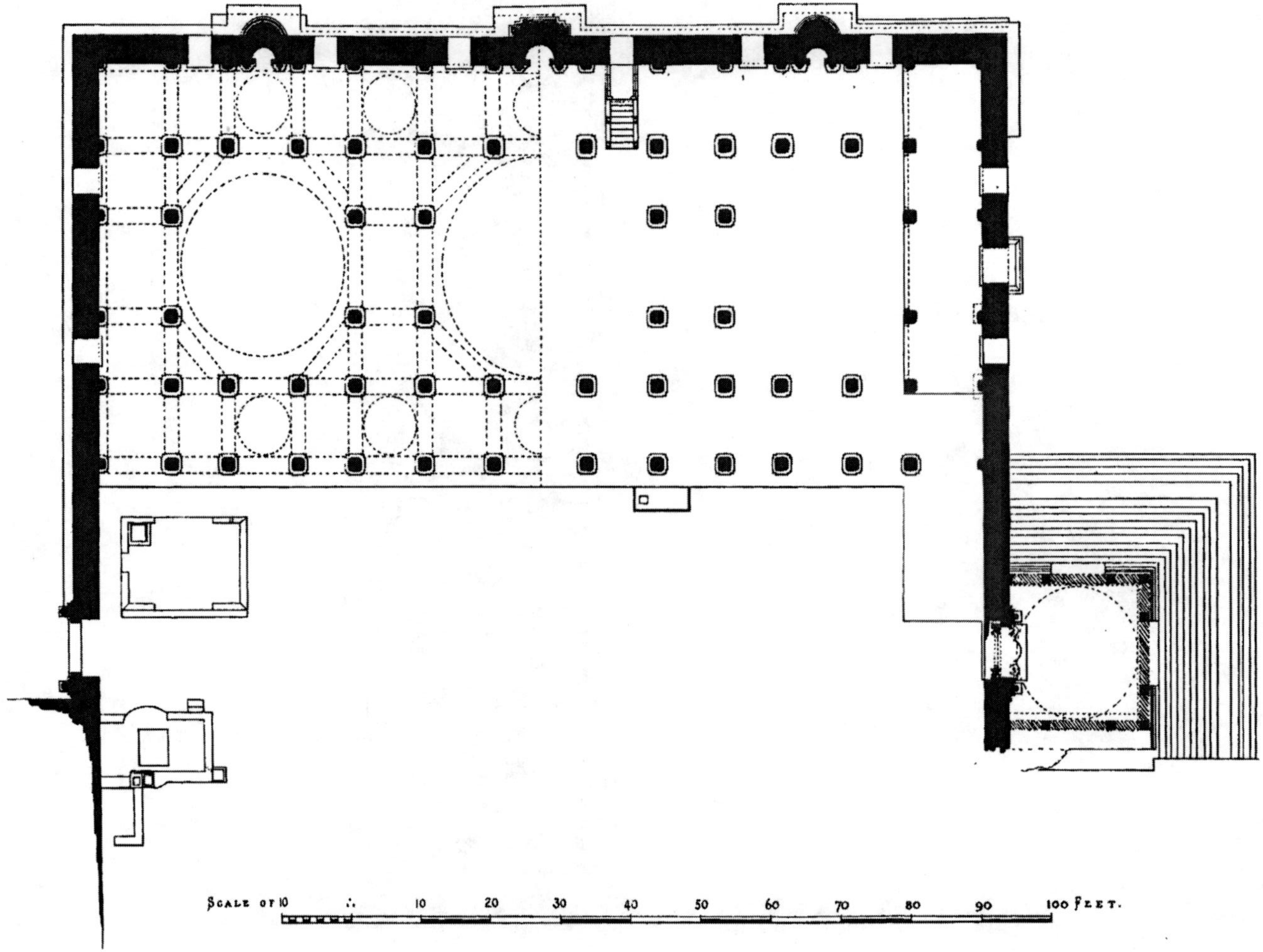

J. Burgess, dir.

H. Cousens, surv.

BHAROCH: FAÇADE [illegible]

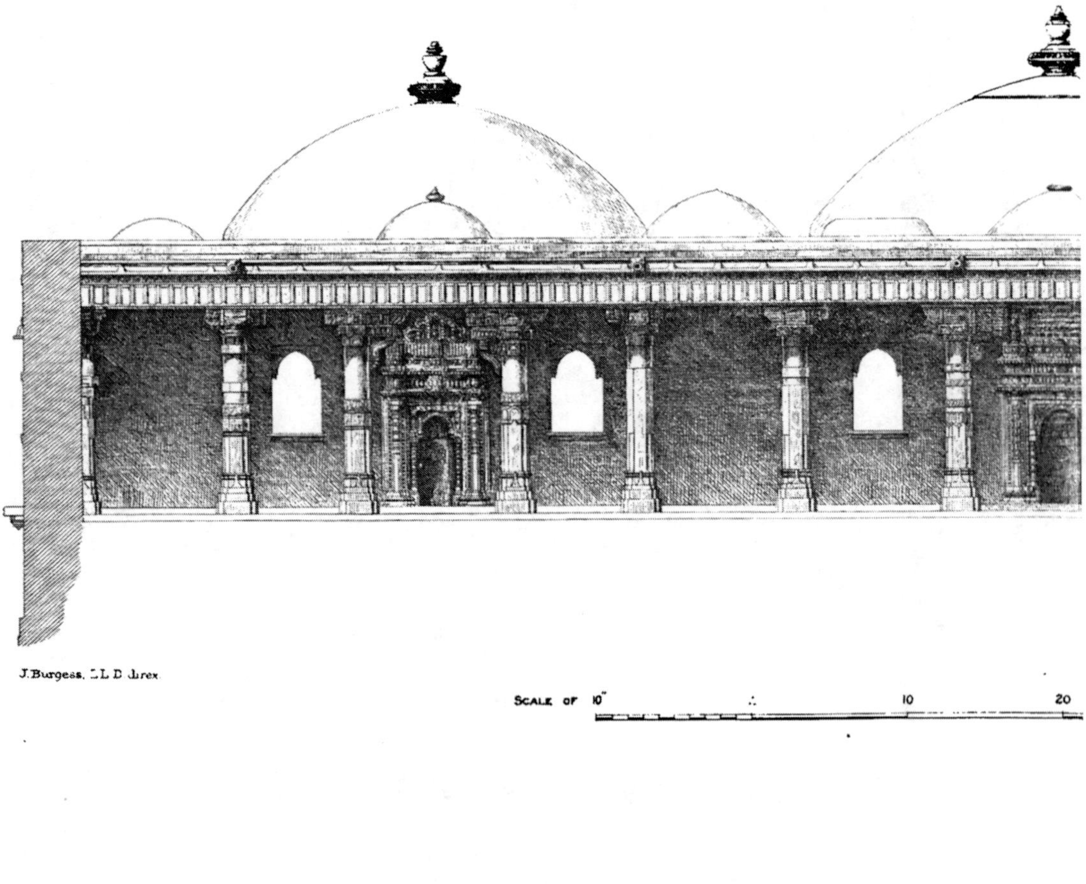

J. Burgess. LL.D. direx.

Scale of 10" [illegible] 10 20

ADE OF JAMI MASJID.

PLATE IV

H. Cousens, Supt.

20 30 40 50 FEET

scarcely possible to recognise the wonderful richness and variety of their patterns—probably unequalled in India.

The mosque is 126½ feet long inside and 52 feet from the front of the façade to the back wall (see plan on Plate III.). The roof is supported by forty-eight pillars, in two rows of twelve each in front and one at the back, with two broken rows of six each supporting the sides of three domes—the central one about 30 feet in diameter and the side ones about 23 feet each. There are also seven small domes, of about 8 feet diameter each, over the alternate spaces in the front aisle, and the same in the back one (elevation, Plate IV.). Along the walls are twenty-four pilasters, or attached shafts corresponding to the rows of pillars. The pillars, it will be observed, are not spaced equally apart, but the second and fourth spaces from each end are 8 feet between the centres of the pillars, the sixth or central pair are 13′ 3″, and all the others 10′ 1½″ between centres. In the rows across, too, the central pair are 12′ 8″ between centres, the back and front 10′ 1½″, and the intermediate spaces 9 feet. Thus the area to be covered by the central dome is 31′ 9″ by 28′ 10″, and those by the other two each 28′ 10″ by 24′ 4″; the irregularity, however, is got over by the aid of the Hindû brackets, and by variations in the projections of the lintels forming the octagon from which each dome has to rise. The smaller spaces have been roofed, not quite symmetrically, by slabs and small domes, torn from some beautiful Jaina or Hindû temple; and when the stock of these was exhausted, plain sandstone slabs were resorted to for coverings to the remaining compartments.

Of these very remarkable roofs, the best are reproduced in the thirteen examples on Plates X. to XVI.,—six being from the smaller domes. The sections attached to several of the more complicated will make the relief more intelligible: description is quite impossible.

The pillars, as will appear from Plates II. and VII., have also been taken from Hindû temples. Inside, they are 14 feet 7 inches high, including the brackets; and a bold drip projects over the row in the front of the mosque. Two examples from the inner ones are given on Plate VII., which clearly indicate their origin: the animal figures of course have been mostly hewn out from the ornamentation.

In the back wall were six windows of perforated stone, now all destroyed, except fragments in two of them. In each end wall were also two, and a balcony window in addition, in the north end.

In the back wall, opposite each of the larger domes, are three *Miḥrâbs* or prayer *Qiblahs* of marble, the portions above the cornice, carved in a style quite different from what is usual in Gujarât mosques—perhaps a little too heavy for good taste, but not inappropriate. The central one differs slightly above from the other two in order to provide a proper panel for the usual inscription. It is represented, with plan and section in Plate VIII., and Plate IX. illustrates the beautiful and rich detail of the side Miḥrâbs: these drawings will explain their form and ornamentation better than any description. The inscription consists of usual formulæ only, without a date. The recesses are semicircular and have a large rosette in the upper part,—above which is the carved half-dome that roofs in the apse.

The courtyard, now in a very dirty condition, had entrances in the north and south walls,—that on the south having a portico on a raised platform, supported by ten columns and two pilasters. The marble door from this into the court (Plate V.) is plainly from a Jaina temple, with the Jina as a cognizance still recognisable on the lintel, though most of the other figures are obliterated. Over the cornice are a few fragments of an Arabic inscription in high relief, but too much obliterated to be deciphered.[1] The general style of this door, of purely Hindû workmanship, when compared with many of the following plates representing similar work executed under Muhammadan supervision, will help to show the continuity of the art of the Hindû, under the direction of his Muslim conquerors. It may even be remarked in the details of the *Miḥrâbs*, Plates VIII. and IX.

Plate VI. gives the back, or street view of the masjid, showing that the floor of it is considerably above the street level, and that it has cellars beneath. The backs of the *mihrâbs* and the windows break the wall at the mosque level.

In the court in front is the indispensable tank for ablutions.

---

[1] If the last signs be the remainder of the figures 701, it might indicate the date of the mosque as A.D. 1302.

BHAROCH: DOORWAY OF THE JAMI MASJID COURT.

ELEVATION

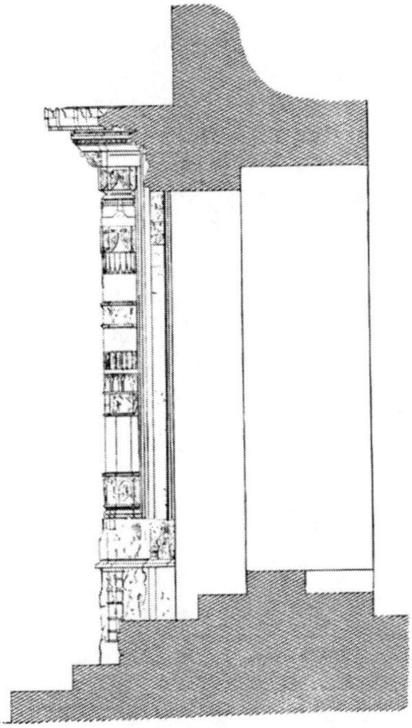

SECTION

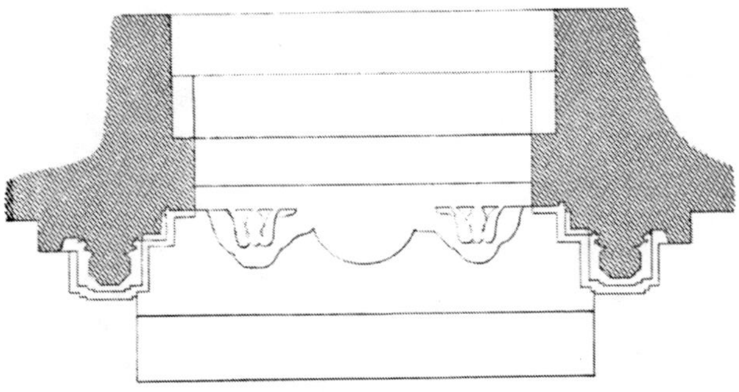

PLAN

SCALE OF 12 ... 1 2 3 4 5 6 7 8 9 10 FEET.

J Burgess, LL.D direx. H Cousens sur.

PLATE VI.

H. COUSENS, PHOTO.

BHAROCH JAMI MASJID FROM THE NORTH-WEST.

BHAROCH: PILLARS IN THE JAMI MASJID. PLATE VII.

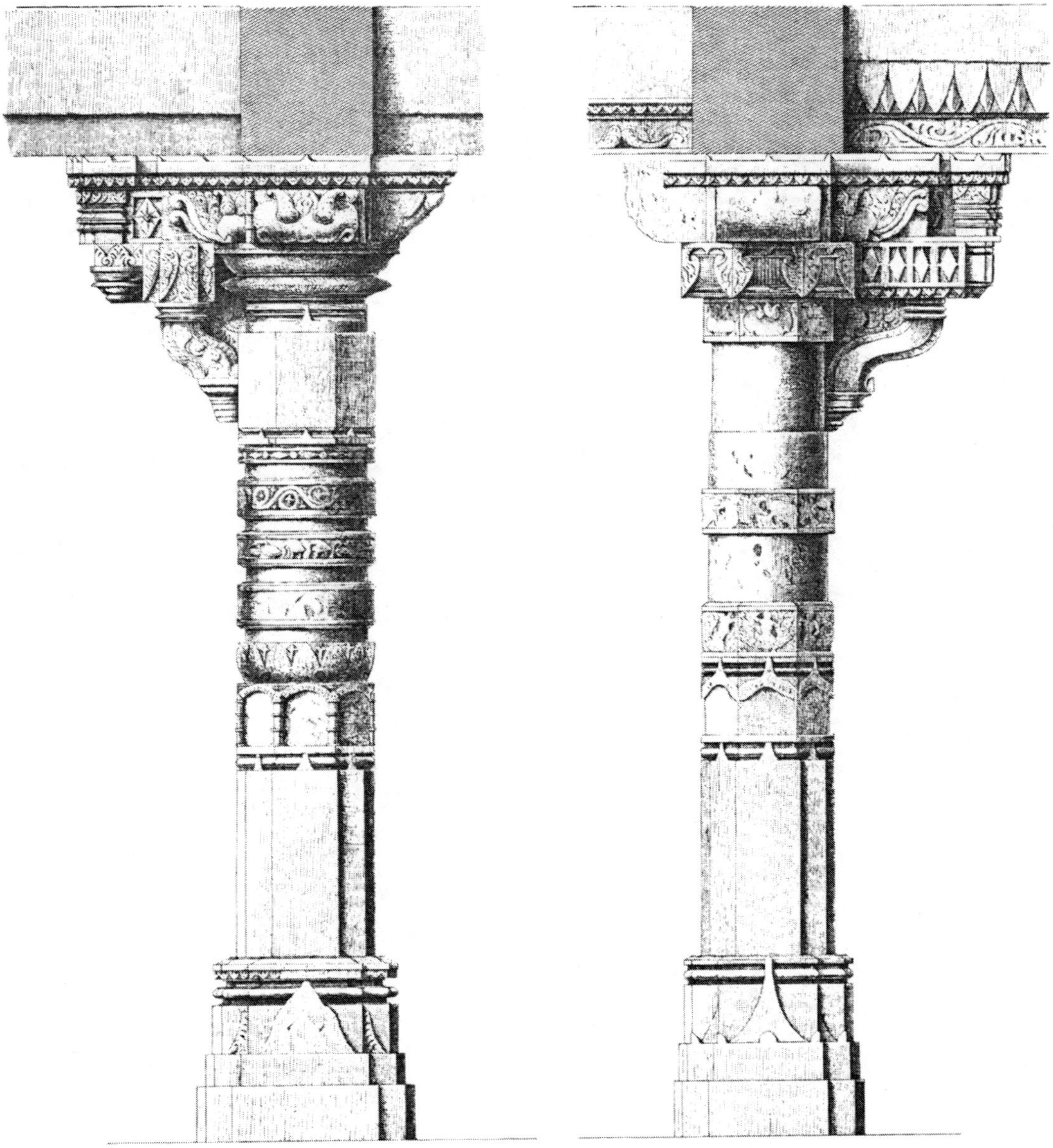

SCALE OF 1 . 1 2 3 4 5 6 FEET.

J Burgess del.

BHAROCH: CENTRAL MIHRAB IN THE JAMI MASJID.

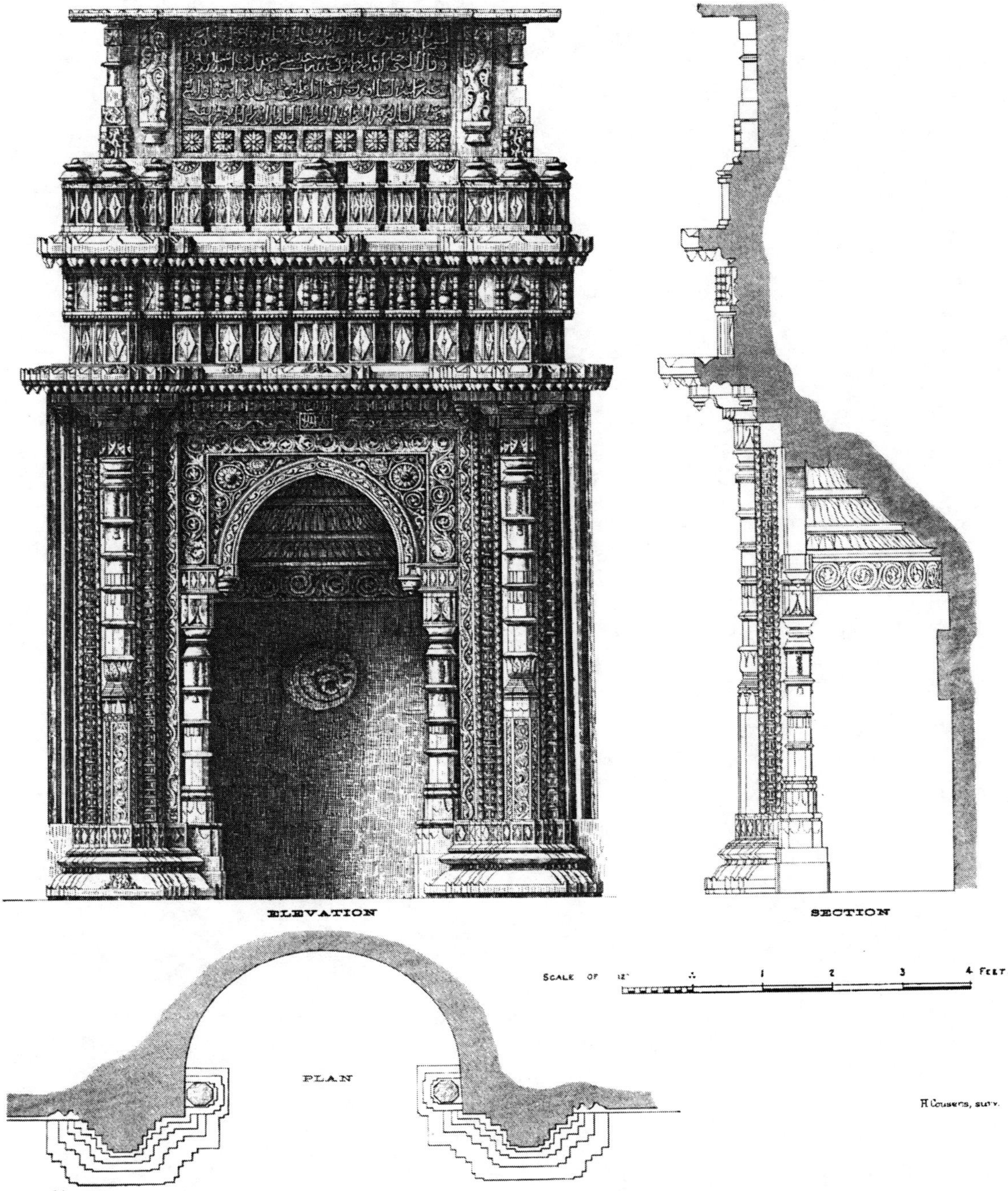

BHAROCH: NORTH MIHRAB IN JAMI MASJID. PLATE IX.

BHAROCH JAMI MASJID: CEILING PANELS.

PLATE X.

SCALE OF 12" 1 2 3 4 5 FEET.

J. Burgess, dir.

Henry Cousens, del

BHAROCH : JAMI MASJID CEILING PANELS.

BHAROCH: JAMI MASJID CEILING PANELS.

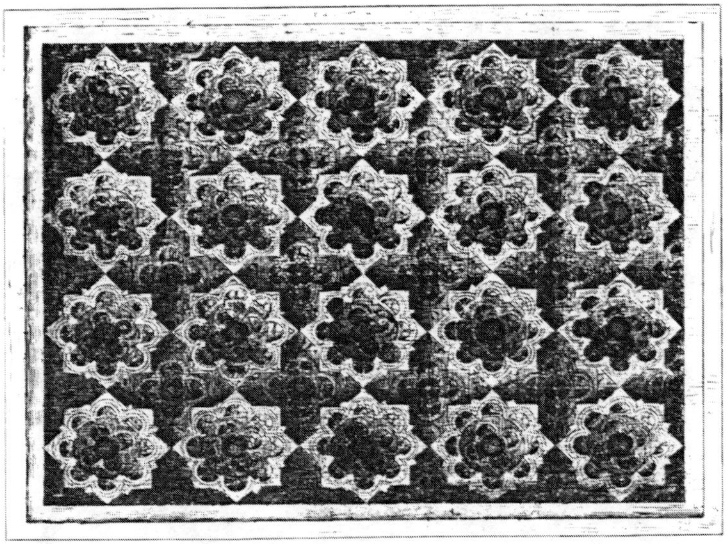

J. Burgess. del.

BHAROCH JAMI MASJID: CEILING PANELS.

SCALE OF 12" · 1 2 3 4 5 6 FEET.

J Burgess dir. H.C

BHAROCH JAMI MASJID: CEILING PANELS.

PLATE XIV

SCALE OF 12" 1 2 3 4 5 FEET.

J Burgess, LL. D. direx.

H Cousens, surv.
H. J. Pachico delt.

BHAROCH JAMI MASJID; CEILING PANELS.

BHAROCH JAMI MASJID: CEILING PANELS.

PLATE XVII.

H. COUSENS, PHOTO.

CAMBAY JAMI MASJID.

CHAPTER III.

CAMBAY, KHAMBHÂYAT, OR KAMBHAT.

KAMBHÂT, as it is usually called by the natives, or more correctly Khambhâyat was known to Marco Polo (1290) as Cambaet, and in the seventeenth century as Cambaia or Cambaya, but in these later days is usually corrupted by Europeans into Cambay.

It is situated on the north side of the estuary of the Mâhî river, 52 miles south of Aḥmadâbâd and about 42 west of Barodâ.[1] In Sanskrit inscriptions and legends it is called Stambhatîrtha, or "the pillar shrine," a name which has not been very satisfactorily accounted for, though it is not improbable that it may have been derived from the liṅga of Śiva worshipped here having had the name of Stambheśvara—the pillar god. In the Prakrits *Stambha* becomes *Khambha* or *Kambha:* hence the modern form of the name. In early times mention is made of a city, sometimes called Gajnî—an important seaport at the mouth of the Mâhî,[2] which was destroyed.

The new city was founded about three miles nearer the sea, it is said, and may possibly have arisen around the settlement of a colony of northern Brâhmans that was located on the present site by Mûlarâjâ, towards the close of the tenth century—the lands granted stretching for eight miles round a temple of Kumârî Devî.[3] The ancient city is now a small hamlet, about three miles to the north-west of the present town, and called Nâgara. It is spoken of as a flourishing place by Maṣ'ûdi who visited it in A.D. 915.[4] The city, famous for its sandals, was then governed by a Brâhman in the name of the Balhara of Mankir, who was full of care for Musalman traders and other strangers. In the twelfth century, it was a well known naval station, with large trade, and protected by a fortress.[5] About that time the Pârsîs are said to have incited the Hindus against the Sunnî Musalmans of the place, and in a riot destroyed their mosque. This coming to the ears of Siddharâja Jayasiṁha, he supplied the means of rebuilding the mosque and minarets. This again was destroyed by some invader[6] probably about the beginning of the 13th century, and rebuilt by Sayyid Sharaf Tamîn at his own expense, with four towers and gilded cupolas.[7]

In 1241, Vastupâla, the famous Jaina minister of Lavanaprasâda and his son, was for some time governor of Kambhât, and founded Jaina temples, Poshâlâs, and libraries.[8] And soon after this (cir. 1310) Marino Sanudo mentions it as one of the two chief ocean ports of India.[9]

---

[1] Lat. 28° 18′ N., long. 72° 32′ E.

[2] *Râs Mâlâ*, vol. I. p. 21; Tod's *Travels in West India*, p. 247; Elliot's *Muham. Hist.*, vol. VI. pp. 353, 354.

[3] On the site of this temple afterwards stood the old English factory. *Bombay Gov. Selections*, N.S. xxvi, *p.* 76 n.

[4] Maṣ'udi, *Prairies d'Or*, tom. I. pp. 353, 354; Rainaud, *Mem. sur l'Inde*, p. 221; also Elliot, *Muham. Hist.*, vol. I. pp. 27, 39, 84.

[5] Jaubert's *Edrisi*, p. 172.

[6] Perhaps from Mâlwâ; the MSS. have Bâlâ, Balwâ, and Mâlû.

[7] Muḥammad 'Ûfî's *Jâmi'ul-hikâyât* (c. 1211) in Elliot's *Muh. Hist.*, vol. II. pp. 163, 164.

[8] *Kirti Kaumudi*, iv. 30 ff.

[9] Yule's *Marco Polo*, vol. II. p. 389.

It was captured in 1299[1] by the troops of 'Alâu'd-dîn; the city plundered; the temples desecrated and wrecked, and the people mercilessly slaughtered, blood flowing in torrents; thousands of maidens and children were carried off; and immense booty in gold and silver, pearls, diamonds, rubies and emeralds, silks and rich cloths, was taken.[2]

Kambhât was then placed under a governor and seems to have soon recovered its prosperity. From a tomb still to be seen, we learn that one Ikhtyaru'd-daulat wa'd-dîn was the treasurer, and died 6th September 1316. Ibn Batuta visited it about 1345 and speaks of it as a very fine city, remarkable for the elegance and solidity of its mosques, and houses built by wealthy foreign merchants, which formed a chief part of its population.[3] The Jâmi' Masjid had been finished twenty years before this on 5th January 1325.[4]

In his invasion to quell the insurrection in Gujarât, in 1346, Kambhât was plundered by the troops of Muḥammad Tughlaq; and in a second rebellion, in 1349, it was sacked by the insurgents and afterwards besieged by the Ṣulṭân. Under the independent kings of Gujarât, it again recovered. Aḥmad I. fostered its trade and enriched it, and, about the close of his reign Nicolo de Conti says it was a very noble city fourteen miles in circuit.[5] "It was still in high prosperity in the early part of the 16th century, abounding in commerce and luxury, and was one of the greatest Indian marts."[6]

In 1535 it was plundered by Humâyun when in pursuit of Bahâdur; and in 1538 it was taken by the Portuguese under Don João da Castro, who plundered it of immense booty and burnt the city. It was again plundered in 1573, in 1583, and in 1606. Still its trade was considerable in the time of Frederici in 1585.

In 1613 the English established a factory at Cambay, and in 1617 the Dutch did the same,[7] but closed it about 1670. In the eighteenth century it suffered the fate of most other towns in Gujarât, at the hands of the Marâṭhas. In 1730 Mirzâ Jâ'far Najmu'd-daulah was appointed paymaster to the Mughal troops in Gujarât, and governor of Khambhâyat, became nearly independent about three years later, and was appointed viceroy in 1737 as Najmu'd-daulah Momin Khân Bahâdur Firûz Jang. He then appointed his son-in-law Zainu'l 'Abidin Najm Khân governor of Khambâyat, which post he held till his death in 1748, when Muftâkhir Khân, the son of Mîrza Jâ'far, was confirmed in the post as Nur ad-dîn Muḥammad Khân Momin Khân (II.) Bahâdur. He ruled till 1783, and his exactions and oppressions, especially his treatment of the Brâhmans, half emptied the city. He was succeeded by his adopted son Muḥammad Quli, the illegitimate son of Zainu'l 'Abidin Najm Khân, and who married Jogni Khânum the illegitimate daughter of Momin Khân II. He ruled well for six years till

---

1 The *Bombay Gazetteer*, vol. VI. p. 216, has A.D. 1304, but the *Tazjiyatu'l Amsâr* of Wassâf indicates the end of A.H. 698 or early in 699, *i.e.* A.D. 1299.

2 Elliot, *Muh. Hist.*, vol. III. pp. 43, 44.

3 Lee's *Ibn Batuta*, pp. 146, 164.

4 See *Lists of Antiq. Remains* (Bombay, 1885), pp. 267, 268; the *Bombay Gazetteer*, vol. VI. p. 216 n. 3, says it bears the date 1308: this is not correct; it is 18th Muḥarram, 725 A.H. or A.D. 1325. The *Imperial Gazetteer* has corrected the mistake in accordance with the *Lists*.

5 Major's *India in the XVth Century*, vol. II. pp. 5, 20; see also Stanley's *Barbosa*, p. 60; Hakluyt, *Voyages*, vol. II. p. 344.

6 Yule's *Marco Polo*, vol. II. p. 389.

7 Stavorinus, *Voyages*, vol. III. p. 107.

PLATE XVIII.

CAMBAY: JAMI MASJID.

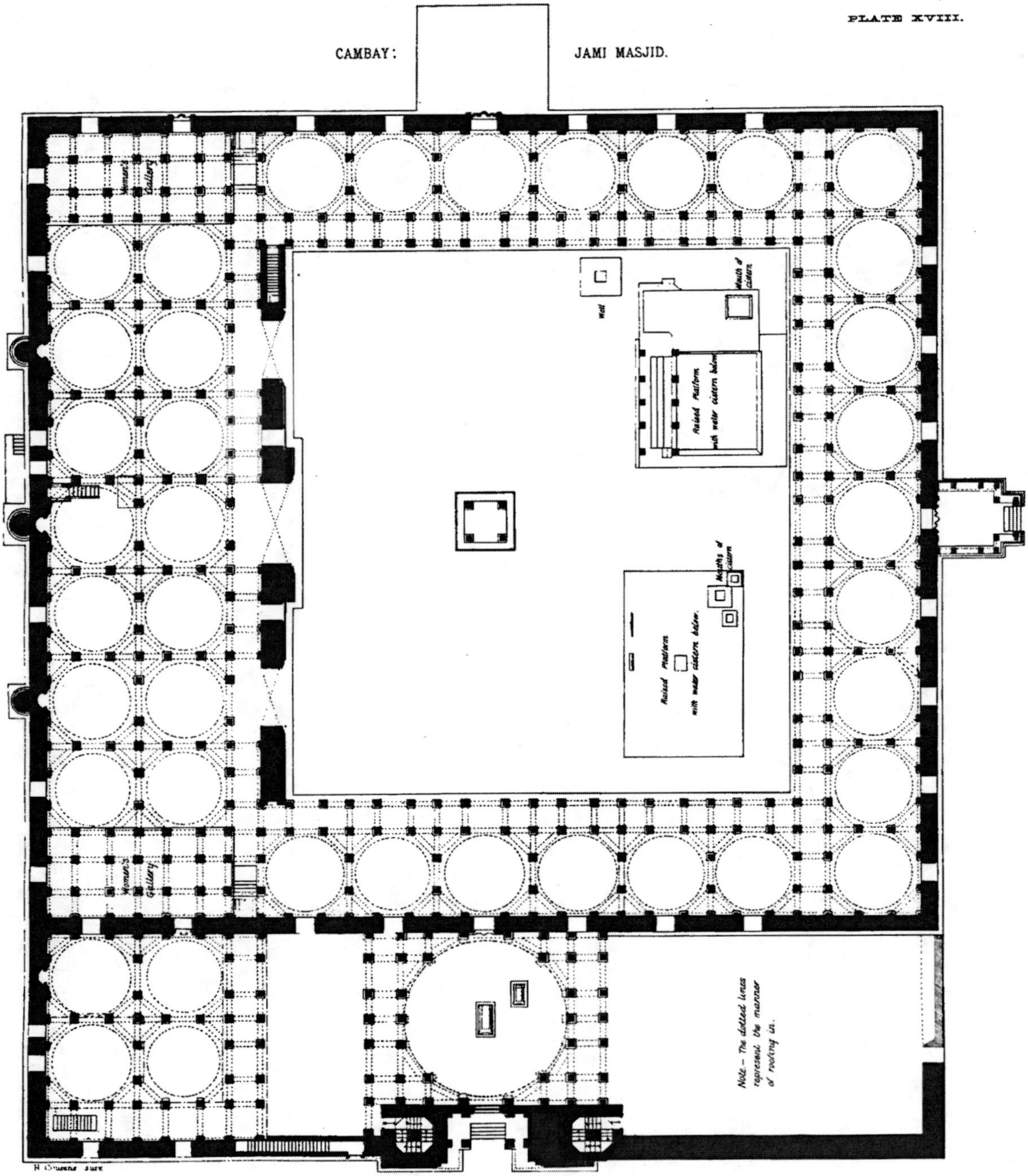

his death, and was succeeded in 1789 by his eldest son Faṭha 'Ali, who received from Dehli the title of Najm-ud-daula Momtâzu'l Mulk Momin Khân Bahâdur Dilâwar Jang, Nawâb of Kambhât, and by the treaty of Bassein (31st December 1802) all the Peshwâ's rights in Gujarât were ceded to the English, and soon after the Nawâb was allowed to farm the tribute for four years, an arrangement which has since continued. In October 1823 this Nawâb died and was succeeded by his brother Bande 'Ali Khân Momin Khân IV., who died in 1841, leaving the state to his younger brother Yâwar 'Ali Khân, but he waived his right in favour of his son Husain Yâwar Khan Momin Khân V.[1]

The population is now about 31,000, of whom 22 per cent. are Musalmans. The trade is gone, partly owing to the silting up of the north end of the gulf, and has been diverted to Surat. The only business is in the manufacture of agates, chiefly for the China market.

The Jâmi' Masjid of Kambhât covers an area 212 feet from east to west by 252 from north to south ; but the south end of this is occupied by a court and tomb, which reduces the length by 55 feet. The mosque itself measures, inside the walls, 189½ feet by 50: the open court in front of it is 134 feet long by 119 feet broad; and is surrounded by corridors, 28 feet deep at the sides and 30 feet in front (see Plates XVII. and XVIII.). The mosque extends across the ends of the side corridors, and its roof is supported by 100 pillars, 15½ feet high, exclusive of three at the ends of each corridor, and by 56 pilasters. They have evidently been reft from Hindu and Jaina shrines, and are arranged in two continuous rows of twenty-six each, at 21 and 42 feet from the back wall, leaving a passage between the front wall and first row; eight rows of six pillars each (with corresponding pilasters on both walls) cross the floor, thus dividing it into fourteen square areas, with the pillars so arranged that the lintels placed on them at once convert the spaces to be roofed into octagons, and these are readily covered with Hindû domes: the front aisle being flat roofed with slabs; but opposite the three principal entrances, this is carried up, as a sort of triforium, above the tops of the arches, and the supporting walls are of perforated stone. Each of the arched entrances is framed with bold mouldings. The jambs of the central one project about 2 feet and, as a substitute for minarets, are carried up to a height of nearly forty feet and crowned with pointed finials. The façade is thus raised in a higher central, and two side sections in such a way as entirely to masque the domes of the roof.

The areas at the end of the floor, in line with the corridors, have each two additional rows of pillars crossing the mosque, but these are interrupted at half the height to support two closed galleries for the women—which were also covered each by two domes,—one in front of the other.

The corridors round the court are roofed in precisely the same way, with a flat-roofed aisle in front, and behind is a series of twenty-one domes in line, the whole supported by 156 pillars and 70 pilasters in the back walls. These pillars are about 15 feet in height, giving the corridors a very light and airy character; and corresponding to each dome is a window through the back or outer wall.

[1] *Bombay Gazetteer*, vol. VI. pp. 221–223.

In the court is a small canopy supported by four pillars (Plate XVII.), and to the east is a very large cistern or perhaps two, covered over by two platforms with apertures for drawing water for the religious ablutions (*wuzû*) before prayers.[1] One of these platforms has a baldachin or canopy over part of the side of it, supported by ten pillars. An inscription on it states that the reservoir was repaired in 1621 by 'Ali bin-'Abdu'n-nabî al Baghdâdi. Such a tank is universal in the courts of large mosques—being quite as essential as the *miḥrâb*, and is simply a copy of what was generally prevalent in the early Christian basilicas or churches of the east. In the forecourt or *atrium* was the cistern or *cantharus*[2] under its canopy where those about to worship washed their hands and lips in token of purification. In the basilicas also, the arcades round the court afforded facilities for groups to walk and to converse, as in the mosques. The façades of the early churches, too, lay on the west side of the court, with their entrances to the east and the altar in the apse to the west.

In a *Sûrah* delivered at Mâdinâh, in the second year of the *Hijrah*, after Muḥammad had broken with the Jews, the followers of Islâm were directed to face the Ka'abah at Makkah as their *Qiblah*.[3] This did not prevent their appropriating Christian basilicas and Jewish synagogues as masjids; and in most cases in India the façades are turned to the cardinal point rather than precisely at right angles to the rhumb-line of Makkah.[4]

In this mosque there are only three *Miḥrâbs* or *qiblahs*—recesses in the west wall—copied and adapted by the early Musalmans from the Christian churches which they first seized and used as places of worship. For this recess represents the *absis* or apse; only Muhammadans using no table or altar the apse could be narrowed in structures built to suit the ceremonial of their own creed, and multiplied by subordinate *Miḥrâbs*, until in later times there came to be one opposite each of the larger floor areas, that is for each large dome. Here however they correspond only to the three larger entrances. They are much plainer than those of Aḥmadâbâd, semicircular in plan; with a pointed arch resting on two side pillars, set within a marble architrave or frame of two flat members, carved with simple floral patterns, the outer one having a sentence from the *Qorân* above, and another on the lintel over it.[5] This is enclosed by two marble pilasters supporting a projecting cornice over which are five blocks carved on the tops like the roofs of Hindû temples and crowned by urns. See Plate XX., for the central *Miḥrâb*.

Behind each *Miḥrâb*, outside, is a semicircular buttress—the central one being somewhat larger than the others. They stand on the podium or basement of the

---

[1] These consist of cleansing the teeth, washing the hands, rinsing the mouth and nostrils, throwing water on the forehead, and washing the face and the feet,—all three times.—*Qanun-i-Islâm*, pp. 72, 73.

[2] Conf. Baldwin Brown's *Schola to Cathedral*, p. 116; Müller, *Archäol. d. Kunst*, § 230.

[3] *Qur'ân*, Sûrah II, v. 139, 145. The first *Qiblah* had been towards Jerusalem, and Muhammad built the first masjid with the *Miḥrâb* in that direction.

[4] The Muhammadans, Hyde tells us, have tables for determining this position called تحويل القبلة Hyde, *Hist. Rel. vet. Pers.*, pp. 8, 9, 126. The strictly correct angle with the meridian at Kambhâyat would be N. 85° 36½' W. Only on a line running north-east through Sirohi is the direction due west. At Peshâwar the direction is S. 73° 50' W.; at Calcutta N. 82° 1' W., and at Cape Comorin, N. 65° 8' W. The door of the Ka'aba itself is on the east face.

[5] On the central *Miḥrâb* after the Bismillah is Sûrah IX, v. 18; over the south one is S. III, v. 16, and part of 17; and over the north one, S. XXXIV, v. 36.

H. COUSENS, PHOTO.

CAMBAY: ENTRANCE TO THE JAMI MASJID.

CAMBAY: CENTRAL MIHRAB IN THE JAMI MASJID.

H. Cousens, surv.

Scale of 12 6 0 1 2 3 4 5 feet.

mosque, and are ornamented with carved string-courses, and capped in a manner peculiarly Hindû in conception. The central one is given on Plate XXI., fig. 1.

Corresponding to each of the six domes (or pairs of domes) for which there is not a *Miḥrâb*, there is a perforated window in the back wall, some of them now much destroyed, but they are of quite a peculiar pattern, and one of them with the string course above it is given in Plate XXI. On each side of these but higher up in the wall are other perforated windows: in all there are eight in the upper tier in the mosque proper and four in the *zanâna* galleries; also one in each end wall.

The *Mimbar* or pulpit occupies the usual position, to the right of the principal *miḥrâb*, and, like most of those not altered by 'Alamgir, it has eight steps, and a small marble baldachin above. For the Mullâ or Khâtîb to enter direct to the pulpit there is a door to the right of it in the back wall which passes on to the basement outside, from which steps lead down to the street.

Along the south side of the mosque area is another, measuring inside 204 feet by 49, with the main entrance in the centre of the south face. This leads into a large domed tomb 39 feet in diameter, with an outer row of pillars on the east and west sides (Pl. XXII.). In it are two tombs—of the builder and his wife—to be noticed presently (Pl. XXIII.). In the towers on each side of the gate are the stairs giving access to the roof: there is likewise a stair in the south wall with the entrance from outside. The roof however of this large and very striking dome has fallen in, and it is greatly to be regretted that no effort has been made to rebuild it. The west end of this court contains the private mosque belonging to the tomb.[1] It is simply a continuation of the Jâmi' Masjid through the partition wall, and consists of two pairs of domes, with the narrow front aisle returned down the left end. Behind the domes on the right is the *miḥrâb*, and on the right is a *zanâna* gallery, with perforated screens round it,—partly ruined; the stone screens in the large mosque have almost disappeared.

The rest of this court is open, and the east wall is now partly destroyed. Doors lead from the tomb, and from the mosque into the large Masjid.

The two tombs in the area, under the great dome, have been sadly damaged by its fall. They were of white marble elaborately carved and that of the man is represented, as now partially rebuilt, in Plates XXIII. and XXIV. The end slab is beautifully engraved: round the outer margin is the first twelve and a half verses of the famous *Sûrah* XXXVI, read to dying Muhammadans in their last agony. In the upper part of this slab, and on an inner border is *Sûrah* II, v. 256,—"the Throne-verse," one of the most admired passages in the *Qu'rân*; and on the base of this triangle, on the left side, is the conclusion of verse 151 of *Sûrah* II, "Verily we are God's and to Him shall we return,"—words constantly used by pious Muslims when in any trouble and especially in the presence of death; and on the right side, the end of *Sûrah* XXXVI, v. 52,—"This is what the God of mercy promised: and the Apostles spake the truth." In the enclosed area is written in beautiful characters, with stems elongated to fill the space, the larger *Kalimah* or creed, —"I bear witness that there is no God but Allah, and that Muhammad is his worshipper and his messenger." Below this, and separated from it by an ornamented band, is an

---

[1] Here again we have an analogy with Christian and even Jewish custom, for the synagogues were often connected with the tombs of the founders, or of local worthies; see the *Itinerary* of Benjamin of Tudela (Ed. Asher), pp. 90 ff.; B. Brown's *Schola to Cath.*, p. 9.

area having on its right and left borders *Sûrah* III, vv. 16 and 17,[1] which contain a sort of paraphrase of the creed; and at the top of the central panel, vv. 163–165[2] of the same *Sûrah*, and under it the Epitaph, which runs thus:—

"This is the tomb of the feeble worshipper, blessed martyr, received into mercy, chief of chiefs, prince of Vazîrs, celebrated in Arabia and Persia, pillar of the state and of religion, 'Umar bin-Aḥmad al Kâzarûnî[3] who bore the title of Zaur-al Malik,—may Allah the most high overwhelm him with mercy, pardon, and the approbation of Allah in the mansion of paradise. He departed to the compassion of Allah, be he exhalted, on Wednesday the ninth Safar, in the year seven hundred and thirty-four" (*i.e.* 21st October 1333).

On the west side of the tomb the upper band contains *Sûrah* XXXVI, vv. 65-71; and the lower vv. 72–79 inclusive of the same.

The ornamentation of this tomb can best be judged of from the representation on the plates.

The other tomb was apparently that of his daughter, but the inscription upon it has been severely injured, by the falling dome: it reads,—

"This is the tomb of one received into mercy, the pardoned, the boast of women, the crown of treasures, Bîbî Fâṭimah who had performed the pilgrimage to Karbalâ. . . . . the deceased Husain, the wife . . . . . . 'Umar . . . . . . departed to the compassion of Allah on the eleventh Shavvâl in the year seven hundred and eighty-three" (30th December 1381). Over this epitaph are the *Tahlîl* or first words of the *Kalimah* "No deity but God" and *Sûrah* LV, vv. 26, 27. Along the sides of this tablet is "the throne-verse" (*S.* II, 256); and on other bands are the *Surat al Fâtihat* (*S.* I.) and the words "O Allah! Pardon this deceased woman, and illuminate her tomb with the light of thy compassion, O most merciful of the merciful!"; on another band is inscribed *Sûrah* III, v. 16, and part of v. 17; and on another, v. 182.

On the east side of the enclosure is a portico supported on eight pillars, with two more in advance at the entrance; they have evidently been taken from some Jaina or Hindû temple (see Plate XIX.). Over this entrance is an Arabic inscription beginning with the usual *Bismillah*, then *Sûrah* LXXII, v. 18, "It is unto God that mosques are set apart; call not then on any other therein with God," to which is added the traditional saying of the prophet, from the *Ḥadith*, "for him who builds a mosque for Allah, Allah will build a house in paradise," and then the statement,—

"This is a *waqf* (bequest) and dedication to Allah. This blessed Jâmî' masjid and place for the congregation has all been built from the private property (*bestowed*) by the grace and bounty of Allah, and offered to Him; may He be exalted! in the reign of the learned and righteous Sulṭan Muḥammad Shâh, son of Tughlaq Shâh the Sulṭan,—may Allah perpetuate his kingdom and his sovereignty!—by the feeble worshipper who hopes for the mercy of Allah—be He exalted!—and for His grace,—by Muḥammad al Bûtmârî (?)[4]—may Allah grant his wishes and guide him! On the eighteenth of Muḥarram, in the year seven hundred and twenty-five" (5th January 1325).

---

[1] Vv. 18, 19, in Sale's version. [2] Vv. 170–172 in Sale. See Lane's *Selections*, p. 30.

[3] Kâzarûn is in the province of Fârs, 50 miles west of Shirâz: lat. 29° 35′ N., long. 51° 47′ E.

[4] Owing to the absence of the diacritical points this name may be read in several other ways.

PLATE X.

CAMBAY: DETAILS FROM THE JAMI MASJID.

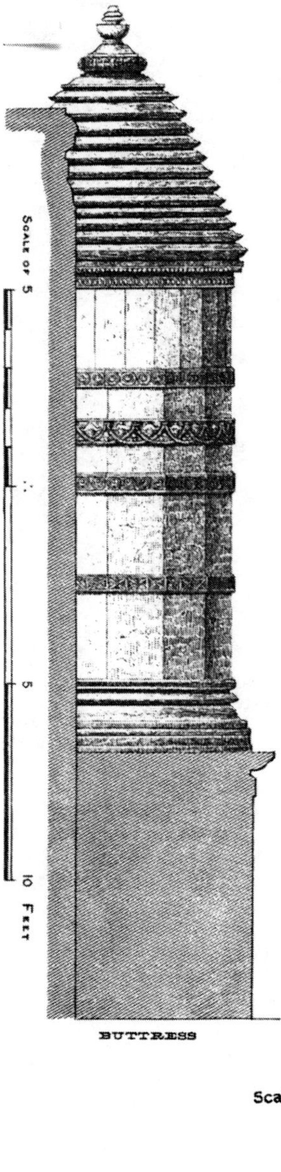

BUTTRESS

BACK WINDOW

Scale of 12" 6" ∴ 1 2 3 4 5 Feet.

PLATE XXII.

H. COUSENS, PHOTO.

CAMBAY: TOMB AT THE SOUTH END OF THE JAMI MASJID.

H. Cousens photo.

CAMBAY: TOMB OF 'UMAR BIN AHMAD AL KÁZÁRUNI.

CAMBAY: TOMB OF 'UMAR BIN AHMAD AL KAZARUNI.

Scale of 12" 6" 1 2 3 feet.

1. FRONT ELEVATION.

H Cousens surv

2. BACK ELEVATION.

On another tablet belonging to an old mosque, we have after the *Bismillah*—"This mosque was built by a servant of the majesty of sovereignty Sulṭân Fîrûz" . . . . And then in six verses of rather poor Persian poetry,—

"In the reign[1] of (*this*) Sulṭân, Zafar Khân Gustarî[2](?) the architect
Built this mosque upright like royalty (*sulṭanî*);
And in the year seven hundred seventy-five from the Hijrah of Muḥammad (1374),
This mosque has been repaired for the worship of God.
May God have mercy upon the worshipper who in this mosque
Utters from soul and heart a prayer for the architect."

In and around the town are several old tombs of somewhat similar pattern to that of 'Umar al Kâzarûnî; one is of Ikhtyâr-ad-daulah wa'd-dîn, treasurer of the city of Khambâit, dated 17th Jumâdâ II., 716 A.H. (6th September 1316). About a mile west of the town is that of Khwâjah Khiḍh'r built in 771 (A.D. 1369–70). The tomb of Hâjjî Yûsuf son of Sayyid Aḥmad, son of Muḥammad, son of 'Îsî, son of 'Abd-as-Sallâm, son of Aḥmad-al Hâjab-al Quaraishî, 13th Rabî' in the year 814 (or 6th August 1411). And that of Fakhr-ad-daulah wa'd-dîn Abû Bakr son of Hasan, son of Muḥammad son of Hasan, son of 'Îsî-al-Quaraishî al-Hakîm, 17th Ṣafar year 818 of the Hijrah (29th April 1415).

On a mosque, in ruins, at the back of Khwâja Khiḍh'r's tomb is an inscription of seven Persian distichs in very elegant caligraphy, dated 1219 (A.D. 1804).[3]

---

[1] 1351–1388.

[2] Or al Shustarî.

[3] For transcripts of the originals of these inscriptions, see *Lists of Antiq. Remains in Bombay Presidency* (1885), pp. 267–275.

CHAPTER IV.

ḌHOLKÂ.

DHOLKÂ or Ḍholakâ is the head-quarters of a tâluka of the same name in the Aḥmadâbâd district, and has a population of about 16,000, of whom about one-third are Muhammadans. It lies about 23 miles to the south-west of Aḥmadâbâd in lat. 22° 44′ N. long. 72° 18′ E.[1] It is one of the numerous sites claimed for the Virâṭa where the Pâṇḍavas lived in disguise. In the twelfth century it was called Dhavalakkaka,[2]—it is said from Dhavala the father of Arṇorâja of the Vâghela clan, from whom the last Hindû dynasty of Gujarât descended. At the end of the previous century, however, it had been adorned by Mainalâdevî, the mother of Siddharâja, with a fine lake which still exists; and, as Idrisi mentions it under the name of Dhulakâ as a chief trading town in his time,[3] it is not improbable that it bore the name long before the time of Dhavala the Vâghela.

It was apparently one of the places at which Vastupâla and his brother Tejaḥpâla built Jaina temples in the early half of the thirteenth century, when, under Vîradhavala, it was a place of great wealth and importance. Under the Musalmâns it was the quarters of a local governor, and the remains of its mosques, especially of the fourteenth century, show that it was regarded as a place of no small consideration.[4] On the conquest of Gujarât by Akbar in 1573 he gave Ḍholakâ and Dhandhukâ in charge to Sayyid Hâmidi-Bukhâri, and next year Wazîr Khân was appointed to the post; and it is often mentioned in the subsequent struggles.[5]

Hilâl Khân Qâzi's Mosque.

The oldest mosque at Ḍholkâ is most probably that known as Bilâl (or perhaps rather Hilâl) Khân Qâzi's, erected in 1333. But who Hilâl Khân, or Mofakhr al Umra Muqarrab ad-daulat wa'd-dîn Hilâl—as he is styled in an inscription,—was, we do not know. (See Plates XXV. and XXVI.)

Inside the walls it measures 142 feet from north to south, by 147;—the mosque occupying the west side of this area, is 35 feet deep inside the walls, leaving 106 feet for the breadth of the court. It consists of five bays covered by five low, plain, conical domes and has as many *miḥrâbs*. The central dome is raised nearly 7 feet above the others by short pillars, having the interspaces filled in with tracery, and the rings of this dome—the section of which is conical—are carved with lanceolate leaves. The others are formed of plain mouldings in concentric circles. Above the first pillars within the entrances, screens of perforated stone are also carried up, as in the Kambhât mosque, nearly to the height of the façade which hides the three central domes. The end domes are on the wings, which are lower and have only a

---

1 The *Imperial Gazetteer* places it on the Sâbarmati, from which it is several miles distant.

2 *Ind. Ant.*, vol. XI. p. 99; *Arch. Sur. W. Ind.*, vol. II. p. 171; *Lists of Antiq. Rem.*, pp. 284, 287, 290, 294, 297, 300. A city Dhavala is mentioned in the *Kathâ-sarit Sâgara* (lvi, 141) as the native place of Chakra, who went on a voyage to Svarnadvîpa.

3 Elliot, *Muham. Hist.*, vol. I. p. 87.—*Dhavala* means "white."

4 See Briggs' *Firishtah*, vol. IV. p. 146; Bayley's *Gujarât*, pp. 11, 145, 228, 237; Bird's *Mirât-i Aḥmadi*, pp. 117, 259, 303, 325, 339, 360, 376.

5 Conf. Elliot, *Muh. Hist.* vol. V. pp. 353, 369, 405, 431, 444, 445; Blochmann's *Aîn-i Akbarî*, p. 397.

H. Cousens Photo.

ḌHOLKA: MASJID OF HILAL KHÂN QÂZI.

ḌHOLKÂ: PLAN OF HILAL KHAN QAZI'S MASJID.

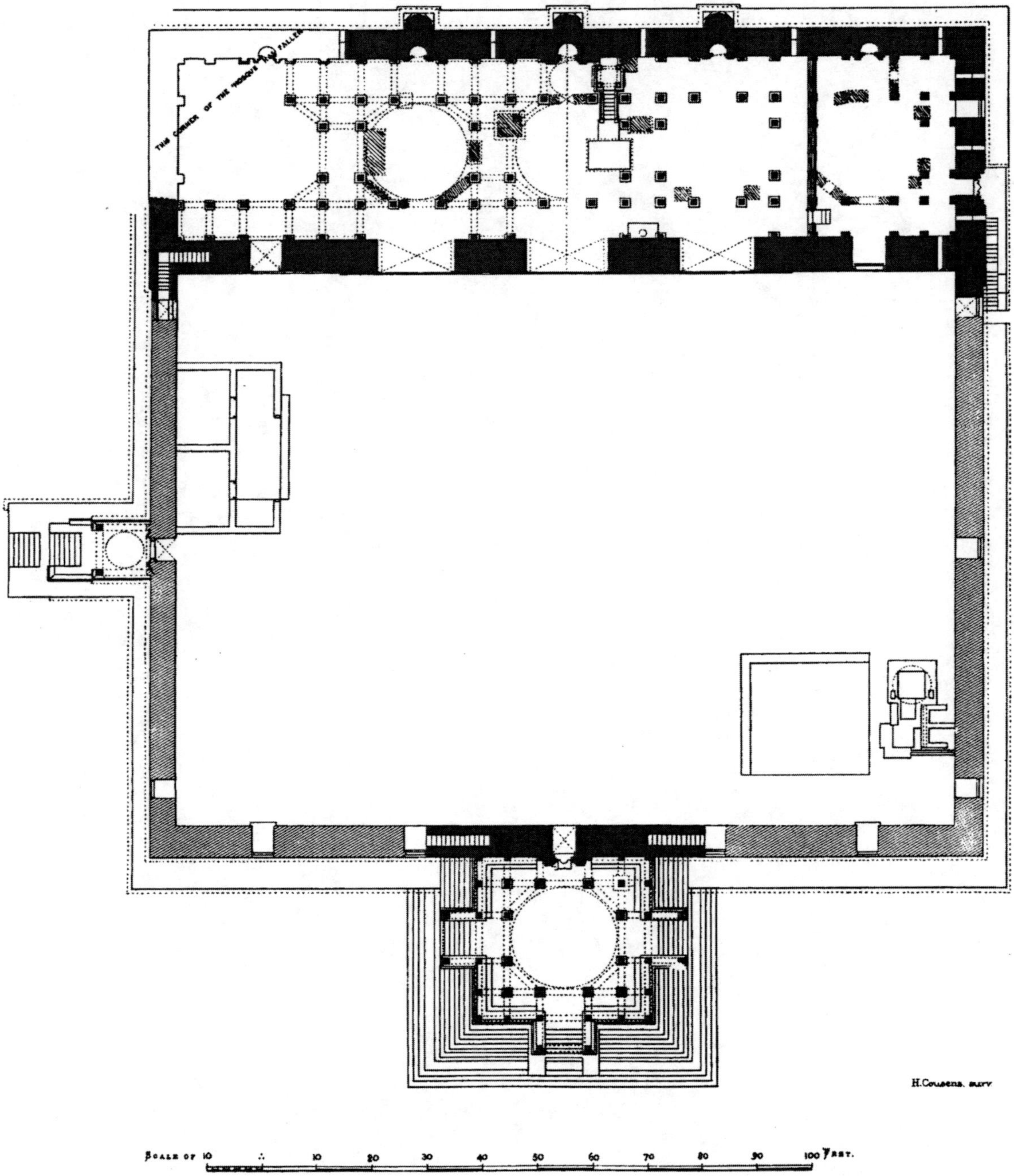

PLATE XXVII.

DHOLKA: SECTION OF THE MASJID OF HILAL KHAN QAZI.

2. TURRET.

SCALE OF 5 ... 5 FEET

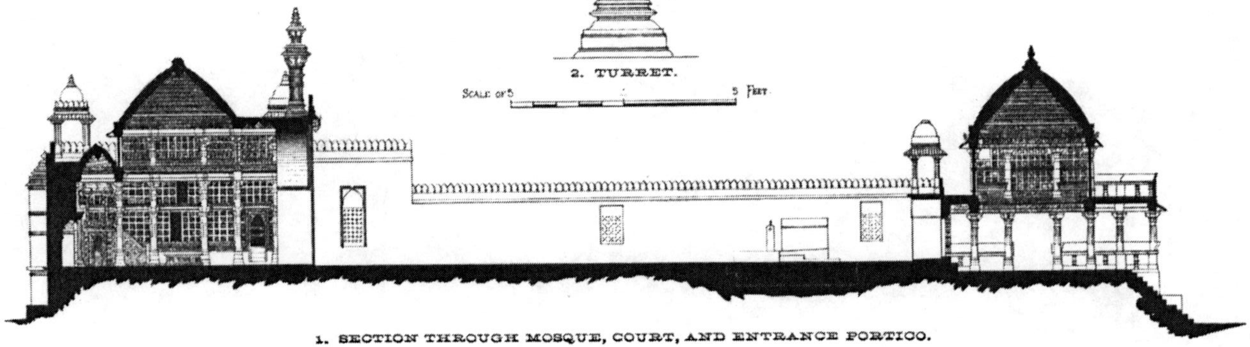

1. SECTION THROUGH MOSQUE, COURT, AND ENTRANCE PORTICO.

H Cousens surv.

SCALE OF 10 ∴ 10 20 30 40 50 60 70 80 90 100 FEET

grated window in the façade of each. The pillars are all plain, and of the usual Muhammadan type, consisting of a shorter or stilted pillar set on the capital of a longer one, the construction being the same as in Aḥmad Shâh's earliest mosque at Aḥmadâbâd. The bases are disproportionately high for the lower shaft. (See Plates XXV., XXVII., and XXVIII.)

The north end is screened off inside, for the women, by a perforated partition from back to front, between the first transverse line of pillars from the north wall. The patterns in the squares of this screen are each a separate device. The floor of the women's hall is raised by 2¾ feet above that of the mosque, and it has a separate entrance from without and a window in the north wall; it has likewise its own *miḥrâb* on the level of the raised floor of the area. This arrangement takes the place of the *zanâna* gallery, and is found also in the masjid known as Sayyid 'Âlam ad-dîn's (or 'Âlam Chishti's) in the Khânpur division of Aḥmadâbâd. The north arch of the façade, opening from this bay into the court, is also closed by a perforated screen.

The south dome has fallen, carrying parts of the back and end walls with it; and, throughout the whole building, many of the lintels are broken and propped up by brick piers. These are indicated on the plan. Plate XXVI.

Each dome stands on eight pillars, and, with the four completing the square in each case, this makes sixty free standing columns in all,—torn from Hindû Temples,—besides the pilasters that correspond. High up in the façade wall, to the right and left of the three archways, and also along the back wall, are formed small ventilators, cut horizontally into the front and then sloping down behind the line of the architrave over the pillars. The mosque being so open they are hardly required for ventilation, and they admit no light. The *Miḥrâbs* are of marble, carefully sculptured, and indicate a sort of combination of the Muhammadan structural arch and the Hindû or merely ornamental one. The Central *Miḥrâb* is given in detail on Plate XXIX. Only the three *Miḥrâbs* of the central part of the mosque have buttresses behind them on the back wall.

The roof just in front of the central *Miḥrâb* is one of those small carved domes in which the courses are carried round in a spiral. We shall find other examples at Aḥmadâbâd. As at Bharoch, so also here, the beautiful carved roof panels have been taken from native temples and placed in the smaller square compartments in the ceilings. Two examples of these panels from Ḍholkâ are represented on Plates XXXI. and XXXII.

The marble pulpit or *Mimbar* is still in pretty good preservation and is one of the finest in India. This, with the small platform in front, is represented on Plate XXX. The face of the rise of every step is sculptured in a different pattern. The sides of the stair are covered with little squares of panelling of geometric designs in deep relief. At the sides of the pulpit platform is a little parapet, sloping outwards, and beautifully carved with little pillars, between which the stone is cut away right through. It is surmounted by a neat canopy standing out, separate from the wall, with a pyramidal roof of purely Hindû design, formed by a succession of sharply cut horizontal mouldings, and supported by four pillars with heavy bracket capitals upheld by struts. The ceiling of this canopy is flat and ornamented with lines of little inverted cup-shaped carvings. The variety of the patterns in the panels on the sides of the structure and on the front of the steps is only limited by the number of spaces to be filled by them.

There are no minârs proper, but two little turrets stand on the front wall,—one on each side of the central arch,—which are quite unlike any others employed in similar circumstances elsewhere: they stand just behind the battlementing of the façade, and are 17½ feet high with shafts 2′ 3″ in diameter. See Plate XXVII, fig. 2.

The two pillars inside the south arch of the façade, have a moulded arch thrown in between them and resting on the bracket capitals of the lower sections of the pillars. Its apex supports the centre of the cross beam above the upper sections of these columns; it has not been inserted to remedy a crack, but is part of the original structure.

The stair to the roof ascends from a doorway in the south wall of the court, and on entering the front wall of the mosque, it turns at right angles and comes out on the roof under a small canopy.

In the north-east corner of the court area there is a tank and urinals near it. Little pavilions crown the four corners of the walls, supported on four pillars; and there are perforated windows through the walls.

The court is entered by doors on the south and east. The entrance on the south has a porch on two advanced pillars, and is led up to by a flight of steps. That on the east is the main entrance and has a fine portico supported on thirty-two pillars, with advanced porches on each of the three exposed sides, to which flights of steps lead up. It is roofed by a Hindû dome raised on the pillars of an upper storey with perforated screens between. This is surrounded by an outer carved parapet following the line of the outer pillars and projections of the floor level. (See Plate XXXIV.)

The door from this porch into the court, given on Plate XXXIII., when compared with that at the north end of the court of the Tâṅka or old Jâmî' Masjid (Plate XLI.), which is purely Hindû, will indicate the source of the design.

The inscriptions which at one time filled the panels over the *Miḥrâbs* have all disappeared, but built into a brick wall now supporting a broken lintel, immediately in front of the central *Miḥrâb*, is an inscribed slab, which, though it hardly seems to fit any of the spaces left, and is carved with incised letters, apparently belongs to the original structure. It runs,—"In the name of Allah the Merciful the Clement. Allah,—be he exalted,—has said 'Verily the mosques belong to Allah, therefore do ye not invoke any one with Allah.'[1] The edifice of this mosque was—during the reign of His Majesty the Sulṭân Abu'l Mujâhad Muḥammad, bin Toghlaq Shâh, and in the time of Malik-ul-Mulûk-ush-Sharq Rokn-ud-Daulat wa'd-dîn-Fattâḥ Sirdâr-'yekdilkhâṣ,—constructed by Mufakhr-al Umra Muqarrab-ud-Daulat wa'd-dîn Hilâl Molley (or Maleki); the architect being the slave 'Abd-al-Karim Laṭif. Dated the twenty-seventh of the month Ḍilhijjah, in the year seven hundred and thirty-three" [8th September 1333].

The Tâka or Tâṅka Masjid.

Next, in point of age to Hilâl Khân Qâzî's mosque, probably comes that known as the Tâka or Tâṅka Masjid,—so called from a water tank which is close to the east entrance. It was the Jâmî' Masjid or chief mosque of Ḍholkâ, however, previous to the erection, in the following century, of what is now used as the Jâmî' Masjid.

[1] *Qur'ân*, S. LXXII, v. 18.

PLATE XXVIII.

H Cousens, photo

ḌHOLKA: INTERIOR OF THE MASJID OF HILAL KHÂN QÂZI.

PLATE XXIX.

DHOLKA: HILAL KHÂN QÂZI'S MASJID.

FRONT ELEVATION

SECTION

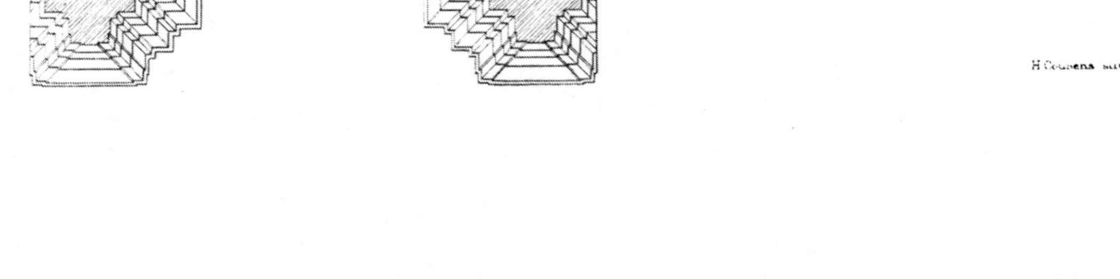

PLAN OF
CENTRAL MIHRAB

H Cousens surv

PLATE XXX.

DHOLKA PULPIT IN HILAL KHÁN QÁZI'S MASJID.

ḌHOLKA: ROOF PANEL IN HILAL KHÂN QÂZI'S MASJID.

Scale of 12" ∴ 1 2 3 Feet.

DHOLKA: ROOF PANEL IN HILAL KHÂN QÂZI'S MASJID.

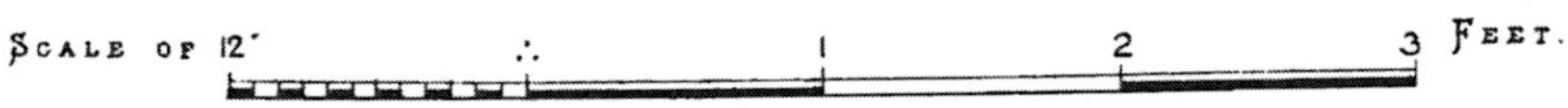

PLATE XXXIII.

DHOLKA: MASJID OF HILAL KHÁN QÁZI.

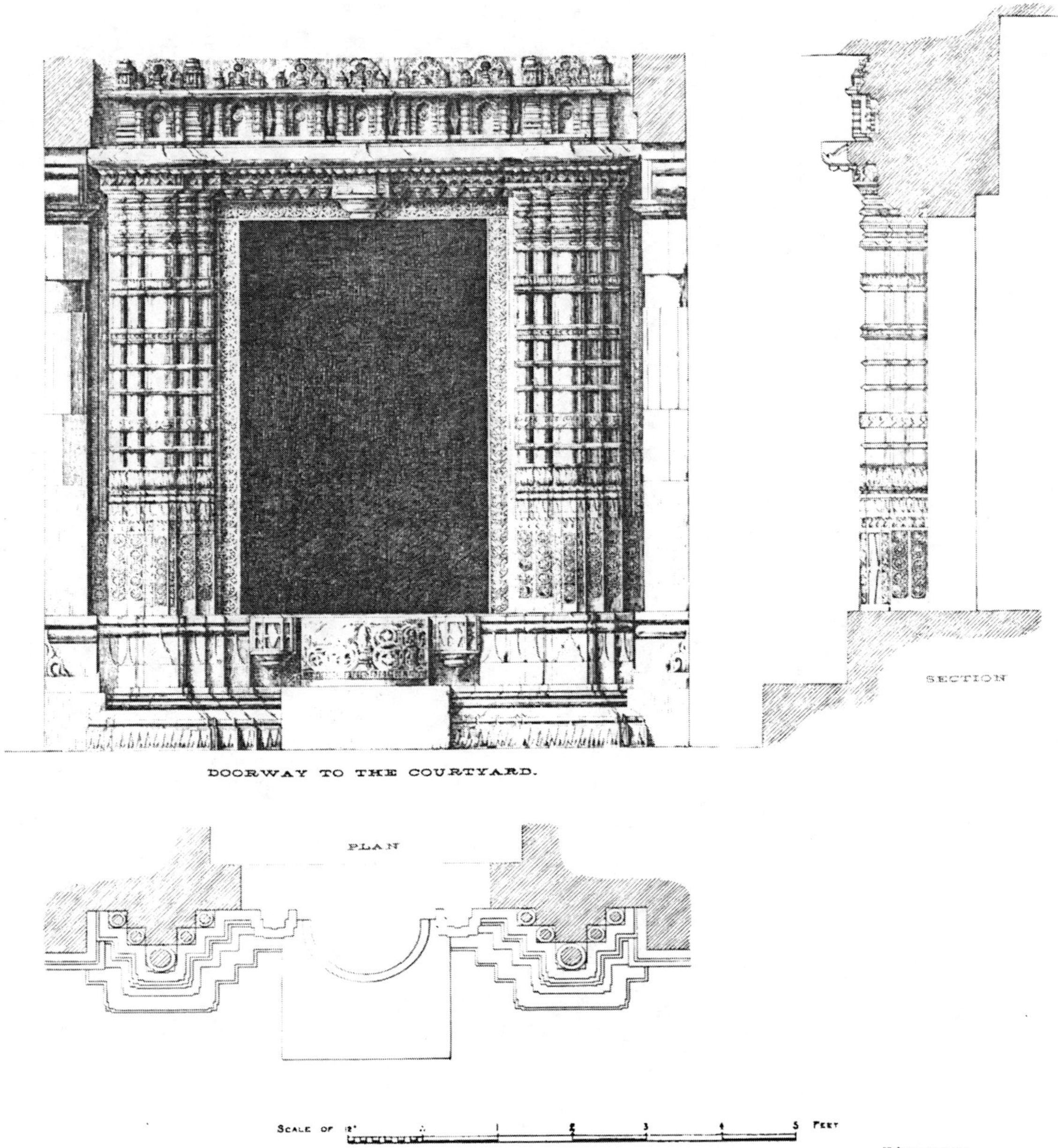

DOORWAY TO THE COURTYARD.

H. Cousens Photo.

ḌHOLKA: ENTRANCE PORCH TO THE COURTYARD OF HILAL KHÂN QÂZI'S MASJID.

H Cousens Photo

ḌHOLKA: THE TÂṄKA MASJID, S.W. CORNER.

About the date of this one, A.D. 1361, there is no room for doubt, for over the *Miḥrâbs*, we have it thrice recorded; first in Arabic prose, and twice in Persian verse. Over the central *Miḥrâb*, after some quotations from the *Qur'ân*,[1] the Arabic inscription goes on,—

"This noble Jâmî' Masjid was built in the reign of the very great Sulṭân and honoured Qaharmân,[2] shadow of Allah upon earth, vivifier of the *sunnah* and *farz*,[3] confider in the aid of the Merciful; Firûz Shâh the Sulṭân,—may Allah perpetuate his kingdom and make everlasting his monarchy,—from the special property of His Majesty the king,—lord of the sword and of the pen, protector of (*divine*) knowledge, and of (*secular*) knowledge, by Mufakhr-al-Khowâṣ âkhyâr-ad-Daulat wa'd-dîn Mufarraḥ-as-sulṭâni,[4]—may his special dignity be permanent, and may the shadow of the (*royal*) portals be extended towards him. And this was on the tenth Rabî'u'l-âkhir, in the year seven hundred and sixty-two" (17th Feb. 1361).

Over one of the side *Miḥrâbs*, is, in Persian verse, the inscription:—

"In the reign of Firûz Shâh, another Alexander,
Mufarraḥ-Mufakhr al-Khowâṣ Khâṣ-al-Khâṣ Sulṭâni
Built the pure Jâmî' mosque in Dholqah
Of his own special private property by the divine favour of Allah.
Upon amber bricks there are roses from musk of Tâtâry.[5]
The mortar is of pure camphor.[6] Bravo to the fortunate builder!
The meadow (*floor*) is like paradise, and men walk thereon.
The five stated prayers[7] are there performed by Maṣ'ud Ṭâyi.
The glorious date at its completion of hard marble was—
Of the Hijrat seven hundred and sixty-two, by divine grace.
Benediction be upon this building of his till the day of resurrection
May all difficulties be repelled and general prosperity ensue."

The other is much to the same effect bringing in "the tenth of the month Rabî'u'l-âkhir," and the year 762, which is repeated three times.[8]

This old Jâmî Masjid or mosque of Mufakhr Mufarrah occupies an area 160 ft. 8 in. by 69 feet within the walls, and has a court of only 36 feet in width by 134 in length. It has a double corridor round three sides of this, with the mosque on the west, constructed of three rows of pillars taken from Hindû temples, arranged nearly equidistantly (see Plates XXXV. and XXXVI.). These pillars are further illustrated by the examples given on Plates XXXVII. and XXXVIII. The roofing of the Hindû temples has also been appropriated as at Bharoch, and two examples more of the carved ceilings are given to scale on Plates XXXIX. and XL., with sections to show the depth of the cuttings in them.

The *Miḥrâbs* are unusually deep recesses, receding about 4 feet from the inner line of the walls, and having semi-circular buttresses behind, into which they enter. An area

---

1 *Surah*, III. v. 16, 17.

2 From *al-Qahhâr*—"the dominant,"—one of the 99 names of God.

3 The *sunnat* are the number of *rak'ats*, or forms of daily prayers in use, as being founded on the practice of Muḥammad; the *farz* are those said to be enjoined by God in the *Qur'an*.

4 مفخر الخواص اخيار الدولة والدين مفرح السلطانى

5 *i.e.*, Yellow tesselated pavement with black ornamentations.

6 Of snowy whiteness.

7 The five periods of prayer are called in Hindustani—Fajr, Zohar, 'Asur, Maghrib, and 'Aysha-ki-namâz.

8 For the texts of these inscriptions, see my *Lists of Antiq. Remains in the Bombay Presidency*, pp. 278–281.

about 18 feet square is cut off by perforated screen work at the north end for the women, having a separate door close to the north wall. In this apartment is a small *Miḥrâb* with an inscription over it, bearing the usual formula from the *Qur'ân* (*Sûrah* LXXII, v. 18). "It is unto Allah that the mosques are set apart; call not then on any other therein with Allah."

In the court a modern wooden erection extends across from the front wall to the mosque and is about 4½ feet wide supported on six rows of wooden pillars. The court, as in the case of Hilâl Khân's, is entered by three doors, on the east, north, and south—each with a small domed porch,—that on the east being the largest on eight pillars and two pilasters. There can be no doubt that this also was taken from some Hindû or Jaina temple, together with the doorway; and the figure sculptures on them were merely defaced. The dome is an elegant one, though it is now repaired with but ill applied brick supports. A section of it, showing the door is given on Plate XLIII. and one of the pillars supporting it on Plate XXXVII, fig. 1. The ornamented parapet round the porch and the door at the north entrance are of similar origin, and are characteristic specimens of Hindû work of the kind in the thirteenth century. The parapet wall of the porch is given on Plate XLII. The doorway at this end, which should be compared with that at the entrance to Hilâl Khân's mosque, is also given to scale on Plate XLI.

Alif Khân's Mosque, Ḍholkâ.

Of the other two large mosques at Ḍholkâ, the great brick masjid of Alif Khân Bhûkâî—known as the Khân-kî Masjid—is probably the older by about thirty years. From its massive style we should be inclined to date it soon after the Rauẓah of Darya Khân at Ahmadabad or early in the reign of Mahmud Shâh Bîgarah. This Alif Khân Bhûkâî was one of three favourite companions of that Sulṭân's youth, who were afterwards advanced by him to the title of Khân and commands of 5,000. The *Mirât-i-Sikandarî* says,[1] Alif Khân "built the great masjid in the vicinity of the town of Dholqah, to the west of the fort. Travellers in many lands are agreed that they have in no country seen so fine a mosque of brick."

There are no inscriptions left to guide us, but there seems no reason to doubt that this statement can only refer to this striking brick monument (Plates XLIV., XLV.). The original façade has long ago fallen, but it was flanked by two square solid towers, the total length over which was 204½ feet, while the mosque measured inside 150½ by 42 feet. It is divided into three square halls by two massive walls 12 ft. 3 in. thick, each perforated by a large central and two smaller side arches. The front and back walls are only 6 ft. 3 in. thick, and the former is similarly pierced by a larger central and two side doors, while in the back, the *miḥrâb* occupies the centre and has a perforated window on each side of it. The end walls have also a recess and two windows each. At a height of about 23 feet, a thin plain string-course runs along the walls and is surmounted by eight arches—four of them with groins across the corners, so as to reduce the square to an octagon—the four on the sides enclosing perforated windows through the outer walls and plain openings through the inner ones. These arches, with groined segments

[1] Sir E. C. Bayley's *Hist. of Gujarât*, p. 228.

DHOLKA: PLAN OF THE TÂÑKA MASJID.

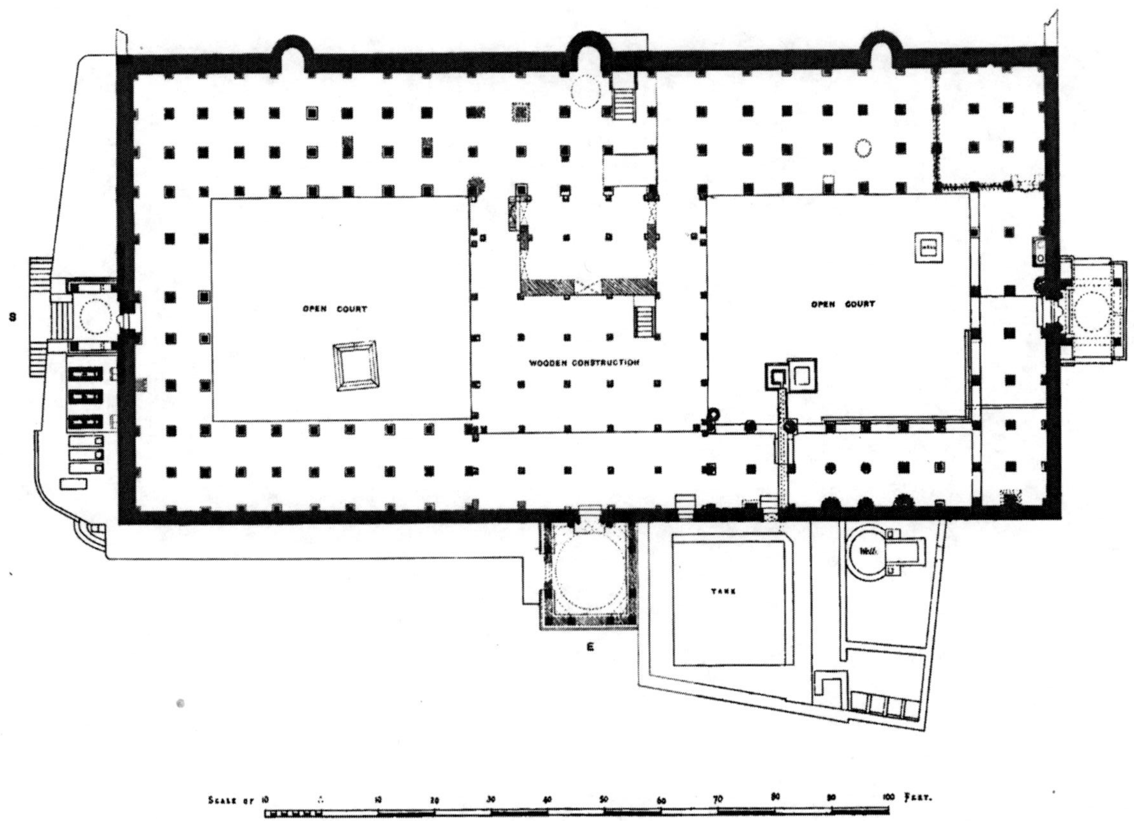

J Burgess. dir

H.Cousens. surv

PLATE XXXVII.

DHOLKA: PILLARS IN THE TAṄKA MASJID CORRIDOR.

H. Cousens. surv.

DHOLKA: PILLARS IN THE TÅNKA MASJID CORRIDOR.

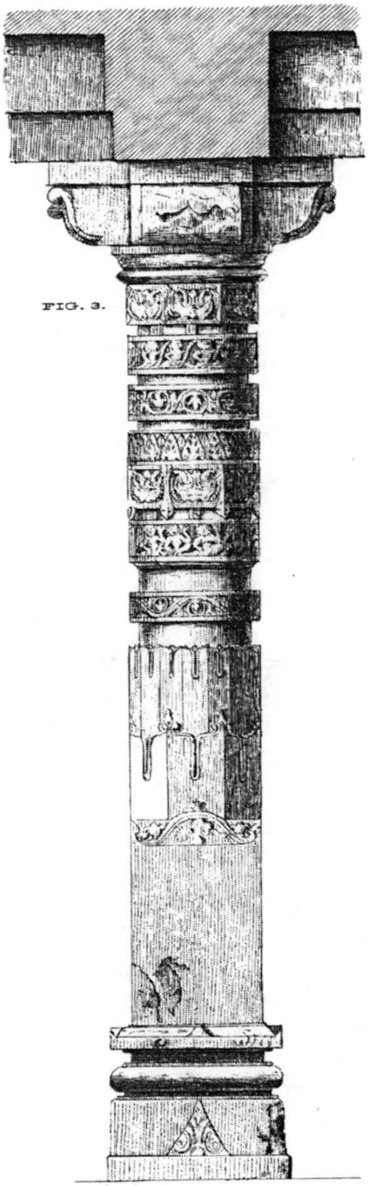

FIG. 3.

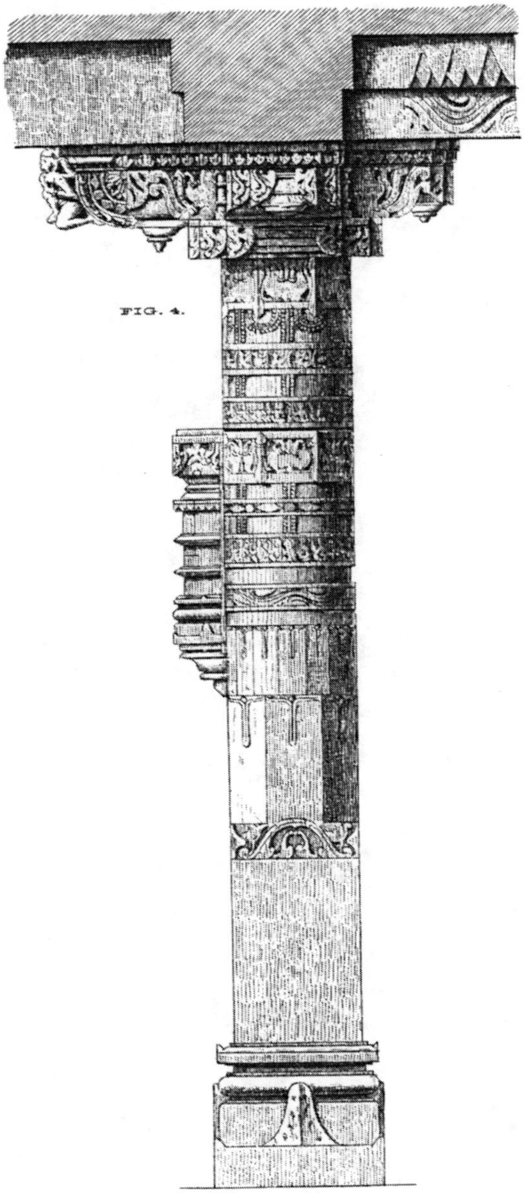

FIG. 4.

SCALE OF 12" . . . 1 2 3 4 FEET.

H. Cousens, surv.

DHOLKA: CEILING PANEL IN TÂṄKA MASJID.

H Cousens, surv

S J Pacheco, del.

SCALE OF 12 · 1 2 3 4 5 FEET.

ḌHOLKA: CEILING PANEL IN TÂṄKA MASJID.

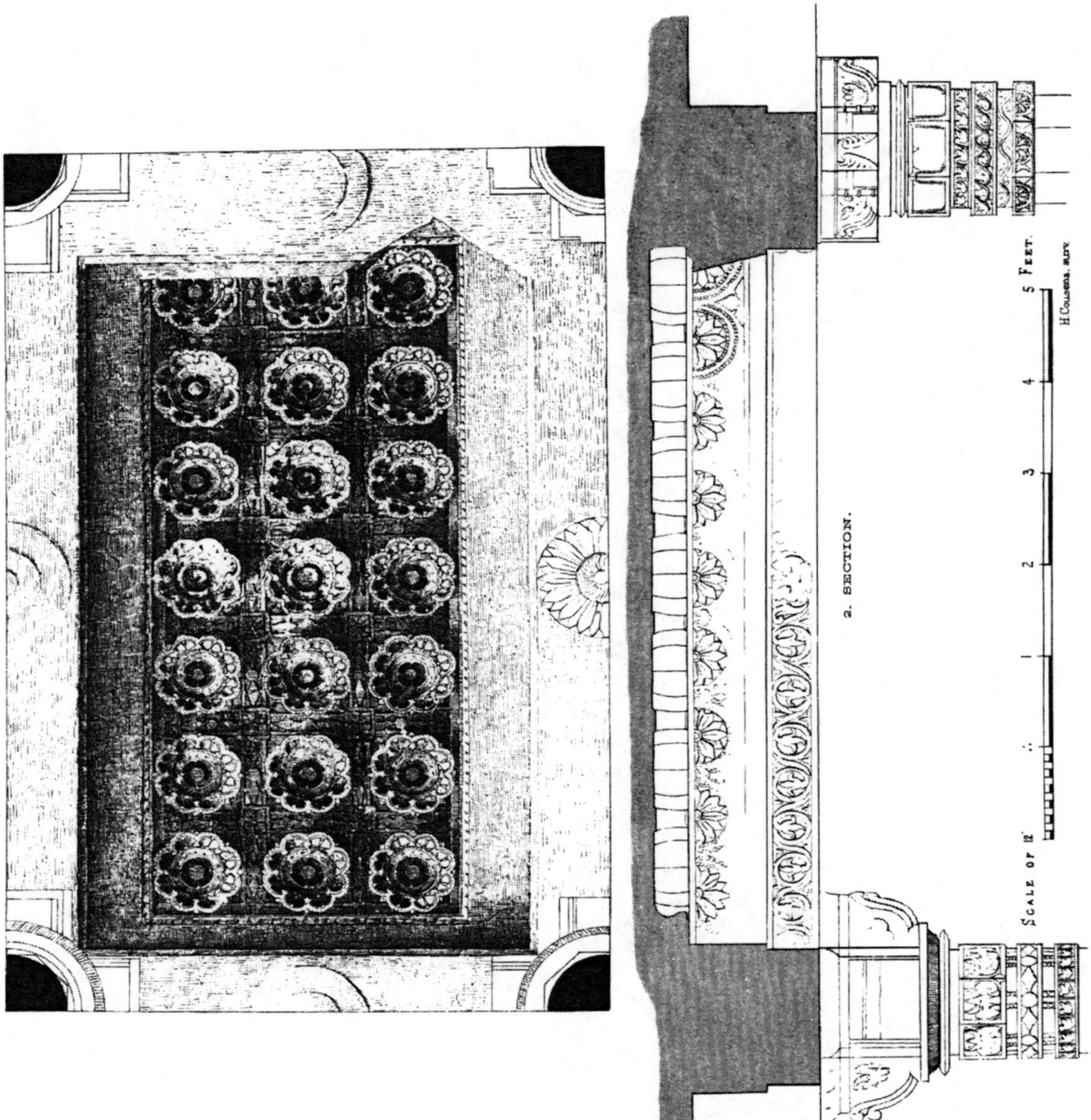

1. PLAN.

2. SECTION.

DHOLKA: NORTH DOORWAY TO THE COURT OF THE TÂṄKA MASJID.

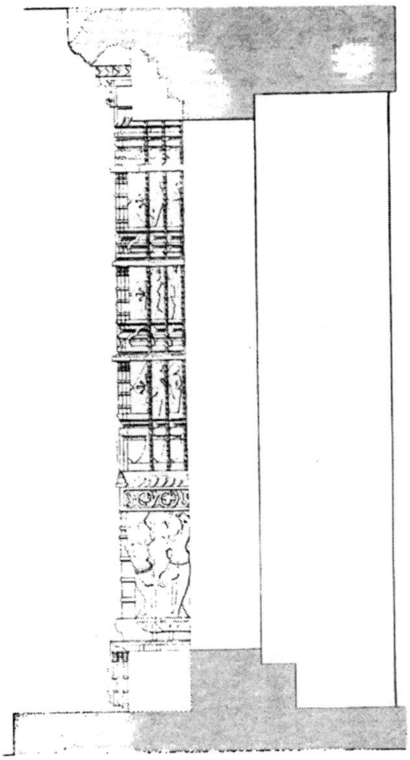

SECTION

ELEVATION

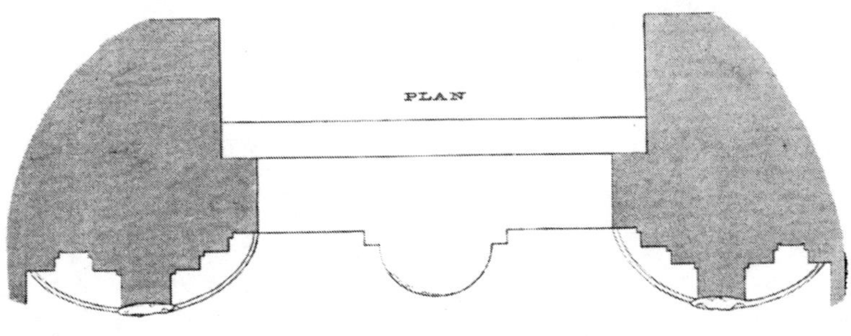

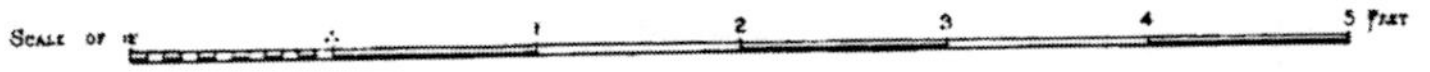

H. Cousens surv

DHOLKA: PARAPET OF SOUTH PORCH OF THE TÂṄKA MASJID.

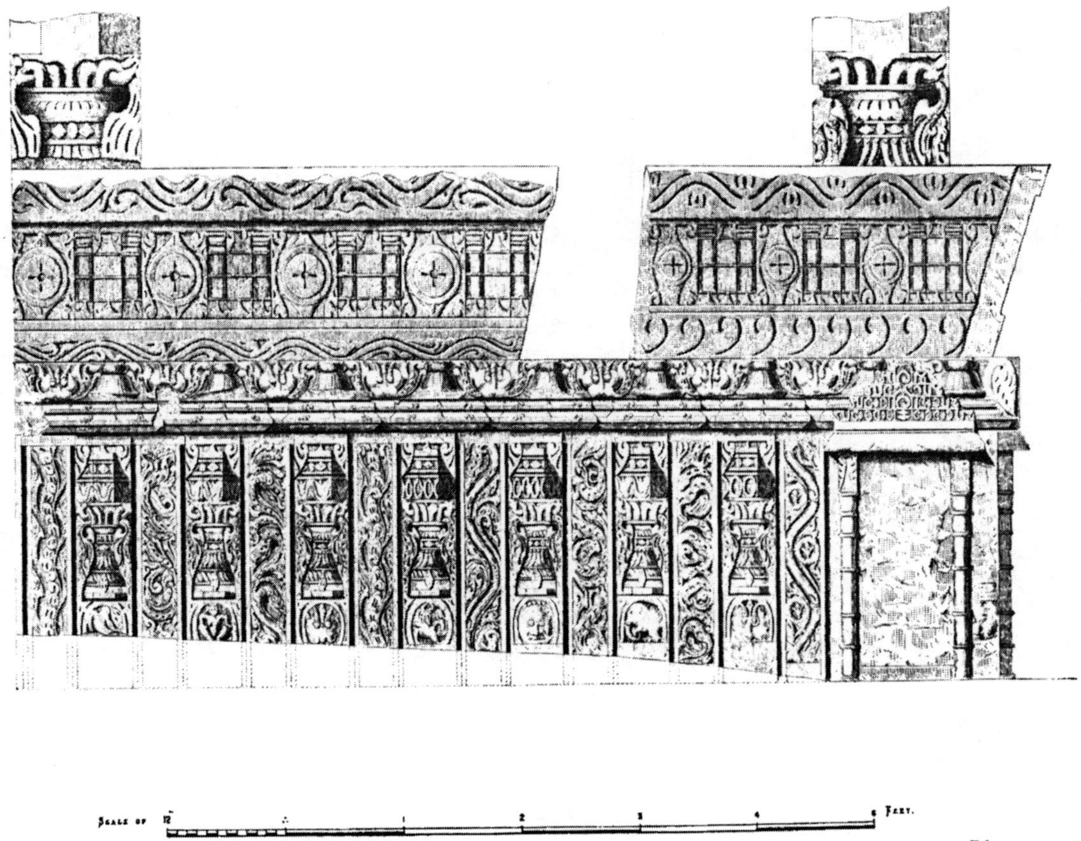

H Cousens, sup

PLATE XLIII.

DHOLKA: TÂNKA MASJID, SECTION OF THE PORCH ON THE EAST OF THE COURT.

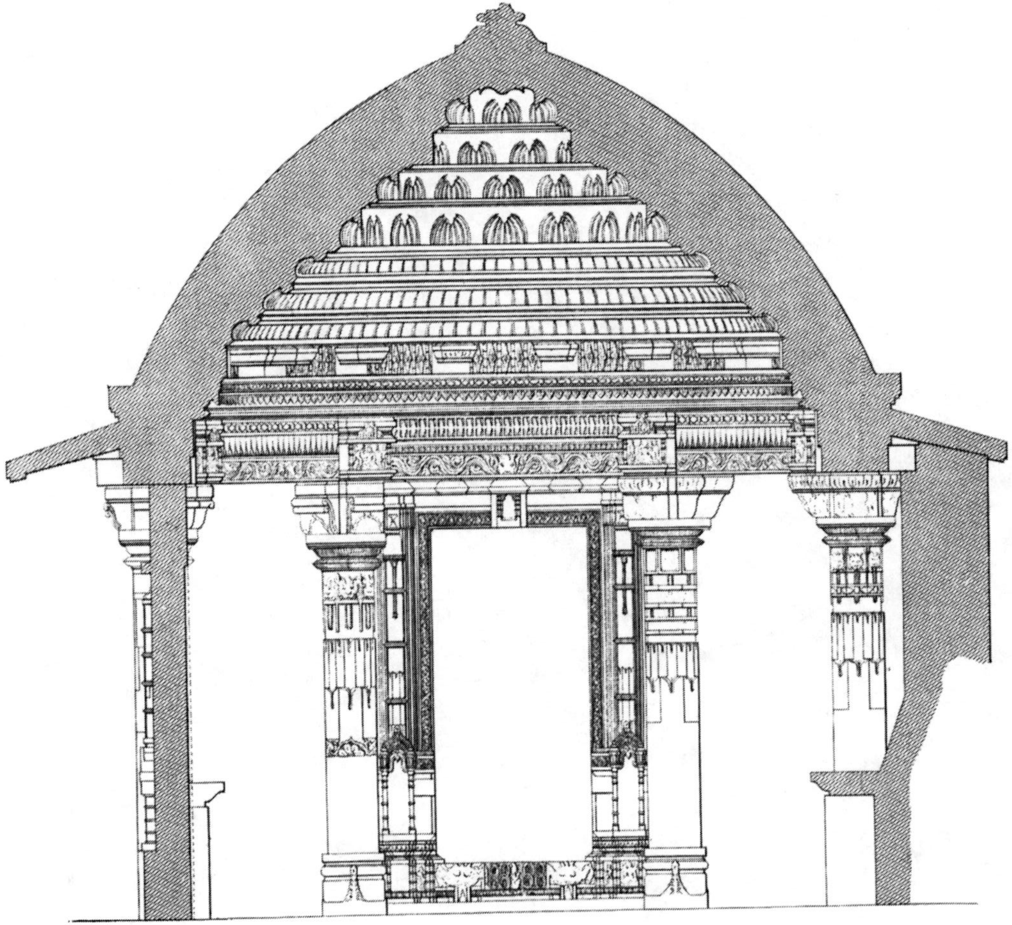

Scale of 12" 1 2 3 4 5 6 7 8 9 10 Feet.

H Cousens, surv.

PLATE XLIV.

H Cousens, photo.

ḌHOLKÂ: THE KHÂN'S MASJID.

between their haunches, reduce the space, at a height of 38 feet from the floor, to a sixteen-sided polygon, with a plain stepped moulding laid over the cusps to form the base of the dome, which rises to a height of 63 feet from the floor inside.

The *miḥrâbs* are deep, being square recesses inside and domed over, with plain façades and doorway arches. In the central hall, on the north side of the *miḥrâb*, is the *minbar* or pulpit ascended by nine steps, with an additional plinth for the platform. Over this is a canopy, supported by two advanced piers and two pilasters carrying arches at the sides. The roof is surrounded by a crown of *kâṅgras*, within which a short drum supports the dome and finial. In front of the pulpit steps is the usual low platform. On the four walls of this room, just under the first string-course, is a belt of boarding about 18 inches deep, and double that over the *miḥrâb*. This was once painted with texts from the *Qur'ân*, which have now almost disappeared. See Plate XLV.

On each side of the *Miḥrâbs* is a small arched window, rising to a height of about 9 feet from the sill or floor, which has been filled in with very fine perforated stone tracery (see Plate XLVIII.).

The whole structure is of brick, but the plaster-work ornament is of great merit, and sufficient of it is still left to illustrate the patterns and the distribution of it. Outside, behind the *miḥrâbs*, are three short half-octagon buttresses against the back-wall, into which the *miḥrâbs* partly enter. The plaster on the side panels and sloping roofs of these is most elaborately ornamented. The central buttress is given to scale on Plate XLVIII.

The entrance doors and windows have also had exquisitely wrought frontispieces in plaster, which are still partially preserved, and the character and condition of which will be best explained by the representation of the north entrance given on Plate XLVII.

At each end of the façade is a solid square tower, behind which—at the ends of the mosque—are broad stairs leading to the roof, and narrower ones ascend from the terrace of the mosque to the top of the towers themselves—a total height of about 79 feet. On them are raised small square canopies for the *mu'azzin*, about 12 feet square at the base and domed over. The towers project 21 feet from the front wall of the mosque, on their inner sides showing the spring of an arch; and cross walls have evidently advanced from the front to meet a great screen with three lofty arches which joined these towers and formed the original façade of the mosque, while the inner wall was carried up to almost double its present height. This wall, however, and all three arches in front with the two cross walls have fallen and disappeared. The whole formed a screen to the domes and hid them from view in front. Under the shelter of the central arch there was a pulpit or *minbâr*, from which addresses could be delivered to crowds in the front court on special occasions. Whether the back wall was pierced with openings above the level of the mosque roof or not, we have no evidence now; but there can be no hesitation about restoring the general features of this noble façade as it must have appeared when complete. See Plate XLVI, which presents this in outline.

At a distance of 303 ft. 5 in. from the present front wall is the entrance portico; so that the court must have been 282½ feet across. The entrance is 20 feet square inside, with arched doorways on each face, the outer one decorated above, like those of the mosque, with exquisite plaster work. In advance of this again, are the ruined piers of a low bridge, that once spanned the monsoon stream which passes here.

Both to the north and south of the mosque, at distances of 63 and 40 yards from it, and near the great Malâv tank, is a beautiful tomb, supported by forty pillars in concentric squares, with an advanced pair on each face—forming small porches. The central square is carried to a higher level and supports the principal dome. The tomb to the north—which is most nearly in line with the mosque—has an extreme length, including the porches, of 61 ft. 10 in., and the other of 60 ft. 2 in.

This mosque of Alif Khân is now quite deserted: half the plaster has peeled off, and it is infested by bees, bats, and swallows. In the north hall a great crack, 6 to 8 inches wide, runs up the middle of the north wall, across the dome, and down the south-east corner to within 15 feet of the floor. Another fissure starts from the crown of the central arch on the south side of the room and runs down the wall. In the centre hall, a crack runs up its south side wall and across the dome, turning down the north-east corner through the upper arch. In both corners of the south side are also large cracks running up into the dome. And in the south hall, one runs up the north-east corner into the dome and circles partly round it: in the north-west corner is another, and smaller ones pass through the upper windows in the front and back walls.

The Jâmî' Masjid at Ḍholkâ.

The Jâmî' Masjid[1] bears some resemblance to Hilâl Khân Qâzi's, but the style marks it out as belonging to the latter half of the fifteenth century, probably not later than 1485, and a comparison with some of the mosques at Aḥmadâbâd of about that date will show many points of agreement. (See Plates XLIX. and L.)

It consists of a central body with three large arched entrances and three domes, —extended by two wings, somewhat lower and having one dome each. The interior measures 100 ft. 8 in. by 33 ft. 6 in., and each dome stands on twelve plain Muhammadan pillars of the "broken-square" type; the shafts are not stilted as in the older mosques; but the two inside the principal entrance differ from the others—being, in plan, stars of eight points and higher than any of the rest. The panel in the roof just in front of these two pillars is carefully carved somewhat after the style of the similar one in the great masjid at Châmpânir erected very soon after this one. (See Plate LXII.)

The other ten pillars round the central area, together with the pilaster on each side of the entrance, support a deep frieze forming a sort of gallery above, which extends back and laterally to the next lines of pillars which support a corresponding series above, rising to a total height of 25 feet from the floor. The inner twelve (including the two higher ones in front) support the central dome, and the outer rows bear the roof of the gallery, and being open between, admit air and a certain amount of light. The side domes rest on lintels only 13 feet from the floor, but with a deep carved frieze over the lintels. The aisle in front however is carried

---

[1] *Masjid* (pl. *masâjid*) is "a place of adoration" (from *sijdah*—"to bend, bow, adore"). From it our word "mosque" has been corrupted. *Jâmî'* means "assembling" (*jama'*—"collected"), and is applied to the principal or cathedral masjid of a city—otherwise called Jâma'-i-Masjid, and "Friday Mosque."

DHOLKÂ: THE KHAN'S MASJID.

HALF ELEVATION AND HALF LONG. SECTION.

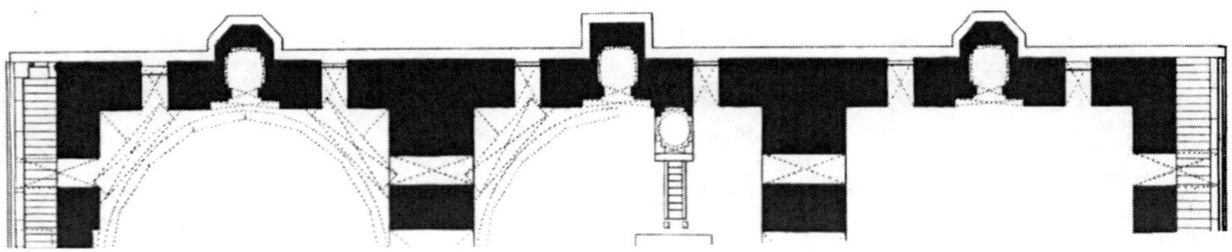

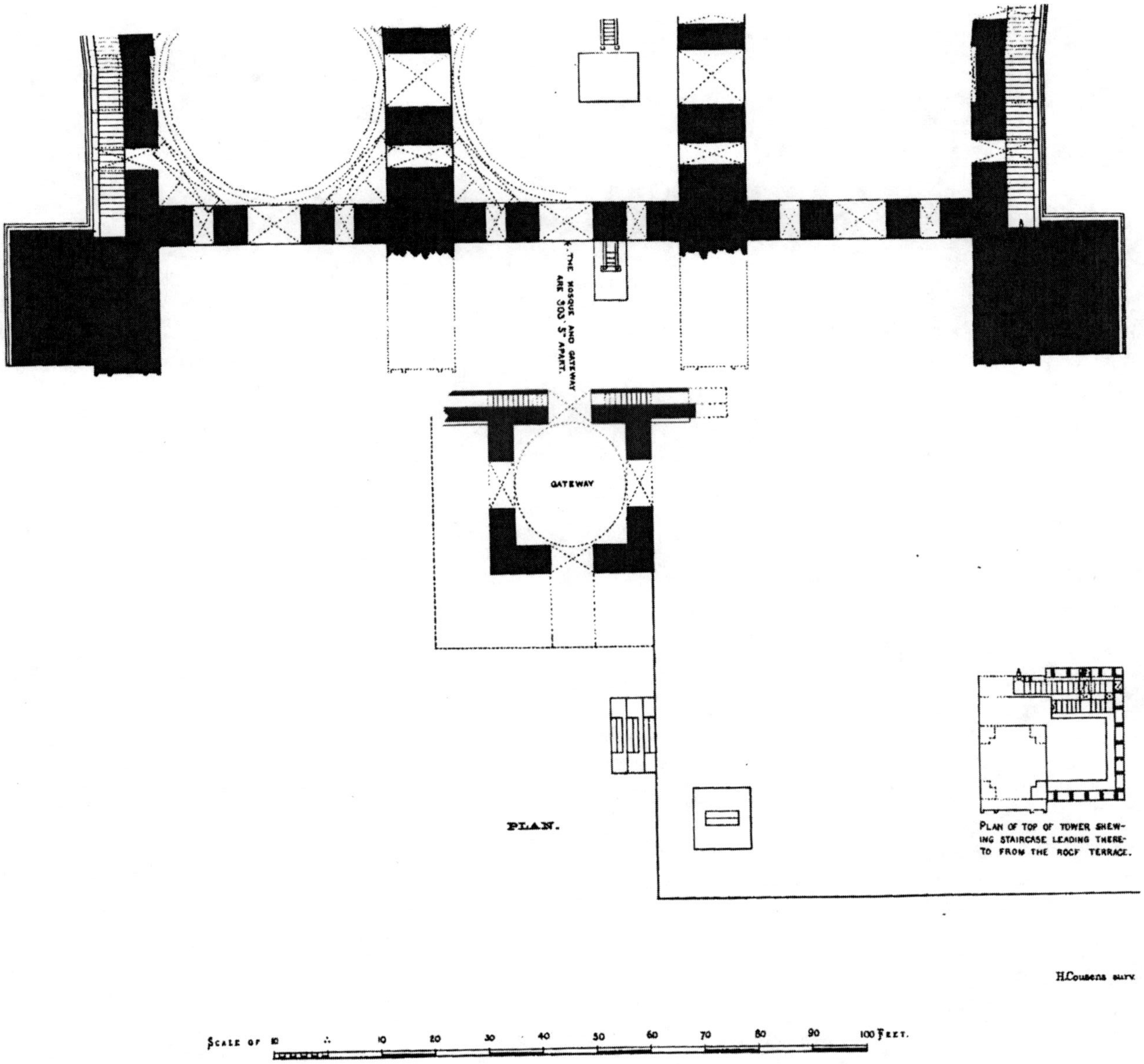

THE MOSQUE AND GATEWAY ARE 303' 5" APART.
GATEWAY
PLAN.
PLAN OF TOP OF TOWER SHEWING STAIRCASE LEADING THERETO FROM THE ROOF TERRACE.
H.Cousens surv.
SCALE OF 10 0 10 20 30 40 50 60 70 80 90 100 FEET.

PLATE XLVI.

DHOLKÂ: THE KHAN'S BRICK MASJID.

RESTORED ELEVATION.

ḌHOLKÁ: THE KHAN'S MASJID.

NORTH ARCHWAY IN THE FACADE.

SCALE OF 10 ∴ 10 20 FEET.

H. Cousens surv

ḌHOLKÂ: THE KHÂN'S BRICK MASJID.

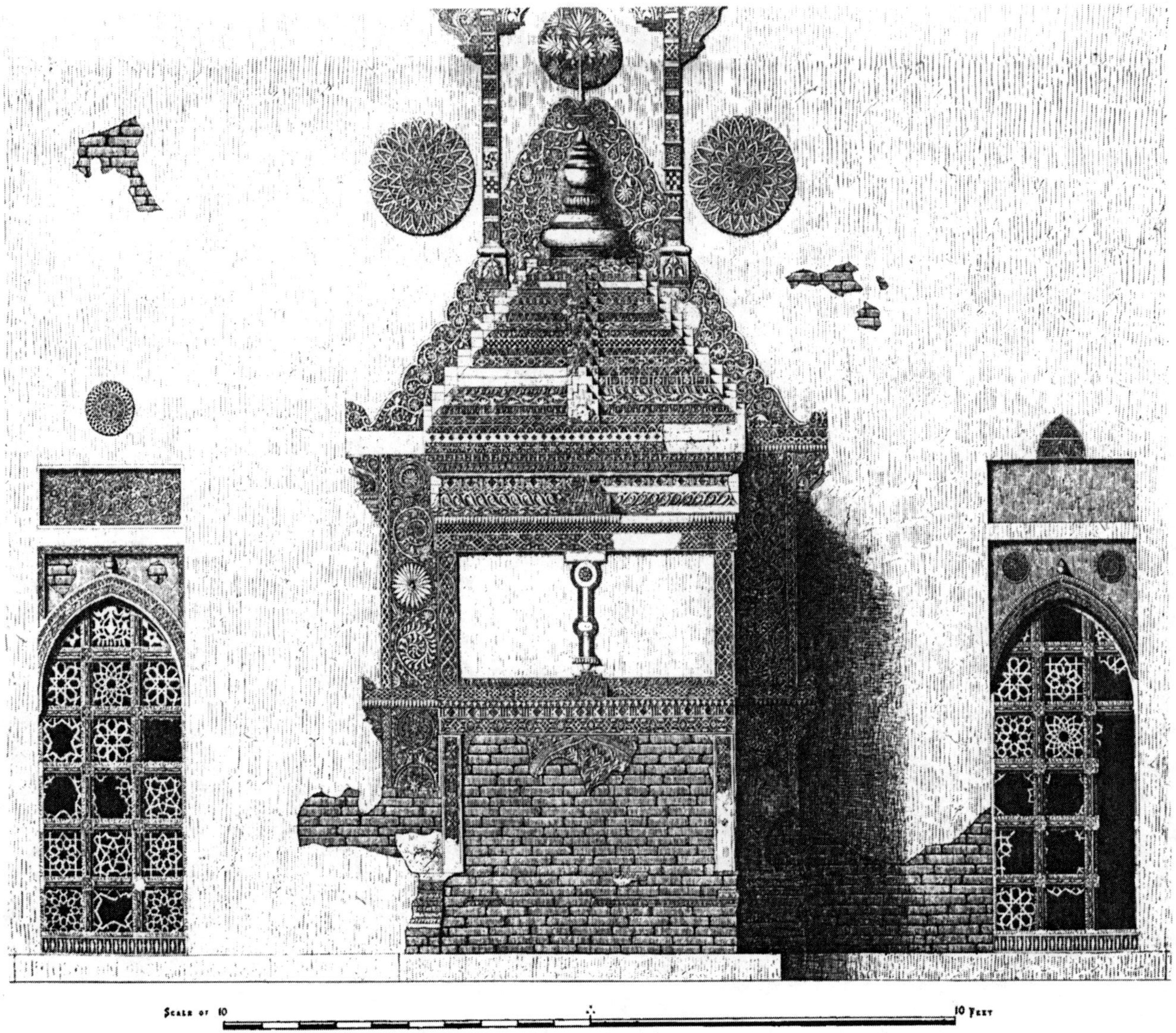

BACK OF THE MOSQUE: MIDDLE SECTION.

H.Cousens, photo

DHOLKA: JÂMI' MASJID.

up, by means of a carved frieze and originally a perforated screen above it, to the height of the base of the central domes. This allowed the side entrances to be made fully 30 feet high to the cusps.

The wings have not this raised roof in front, and consequently the front walls were not required to be carried higher than 17 feet, if the domes behind were not to be hidden. Each wing has only a small entrance door in front.

In the back wall are six windows that have been filled with perforated work. There are also three in each of the end walls but all of them have been more or less broken. The central and larger one in the south end is represented to scale on Plate LI.

The upper storeys of the two minars have fallen. They stand between the main entrance and the two side ones, and still rise in three storeys to a height of 37 feet, having projecting eaves supported by brackets at the top of each storey—the second being in line with the weather board of the façade, which projects about 20 inches from the wall, and is supported by neatly wrought corbels. The upper portions have fallen. In line with the first weather moulding, which is at the same level as the top of the wings, a broad carved string-course is carried across the façades.

The plan of the minars is the well known one of the shrines of Hindû temples,—namely, a square with narrower facets laid upon it, so as to "step off" all corners by a series of vertical rebatements.[1] They have numerous horizontal mouldings; and on each of the three faces in the first and second storeys are niches, in imitation of those for images on the back and side walls of Hindû shrines, but which in mosques are always ornamented with some intricate floral design on the back with an arch within the jambs. Those here are distinctly different from the designs most prevalent at Aḥmadâbâd. As examples from this mosque three of these niches (figs. 1, 2, and 4) from the sides of the minars and one (fig. 3) from the front are represented in Plates LII. and LIII.

The stairs leading up to the gallery and roof enter in the thickness of the front wall in the jambs of the central entrance and turn into the minars a short distance up.

The five *miḥrâbs*[2] in the back wall, are much alike in general style, but with differences in the details, the central or principal one being the richest in carving. It is represented in elevation, plan, and section to scale on Plate LIV. The pulpit or *mimbar*[3] bears a close resemblance to that in the Hilâl Khân Qâzi mosque, but is scarcely so well executed.

As in many of the later masjids, there is no *zanâna* gallery in this. The older mosques nearly all have it.

The court measures 149 feet in length by 76 feet broad, and has an open tank at the south end, and a covered one with two well openings near the middle. In the north-east corner is a tomb, which once had a dome supported on twelve pillars, but the roof is now gone. Three graves occupy the floor.

---

1 *Arch. Sur. Wn. Ind.*, vol. III. p. 21.

2 *Miḥrâb* (plur. *maḥârib*), as already explained (p. 26), is the representative of the *absis* in the early Christian basilicas; they were introduced, in the form that has become general since, by the Khalîfah al-Walîd in A.H. 90 (A.D. 709). In the *Qur'ân* the word is used in the sense of a "chamber" (Sûrah III, 32, 33; XIX, 12; XXXIV, 12; XXXVIII, 20).

3 *Minbar* (usually pronounced *mimbar*), the pulpit, from which the *Khuṭbah* or sermon is recited. In Persia and elsewhere it consists of only three steps, sometimes of wood and moveable, but in Egypt and India they are often more elevated and elaborate structures. Some in Gujarât are handsomely carved. It is said that Aurangzeb objected to the high pulpits as heterodox and had most of them removed for the low three steps of earliest date.

There is also a portion of an old Hindû or Jaina temple 40 ft. by 27 ft., being an open portico, with forty pillars supporting two domes, which has also been converted into a rude mosque by simply constructing a *miḥrâb* in the west end of it. Probably the outer line of pillars also were at one time filled in by a brick wall,—now mostly gone.

Hazrat Khan's Tomb.

Further there is a large, but comparatively modern, enclosure about 465 feet in length by 355 at its greatest breadth. The plan is given on Plate LV. In the centre is the tomb or Rauẓah[1] of Hajrat Khân, about 57 feet square, supported by eight piers, with a room in the centre 21 feet square inside. But it is not of much architectural interest. To the west of it is a small mosque 52 feet long by 18 feet deep with nine small *miḥrâbs*. There is another smaller tomb to the south-east of the principal one, and other buildings round the area, which contain many graves scattered about.

[1] Tombs of notable Muhammadans are sometimes so called from *ar-Rauẓah*—"the garden," in which is situated the tomb of Muhammad at Madînah. In India the larger mausolea are usually called *Dargâhs*,—a Persian term meaning "palace" or "court." The grave is called *qabr*, and as the Muhammadans bury so as to allow the body to lie with the face towards Makkah, in India the graves are dug from north to south.

ḌHOLKÁ JÁMI' MASJID: PLAN.

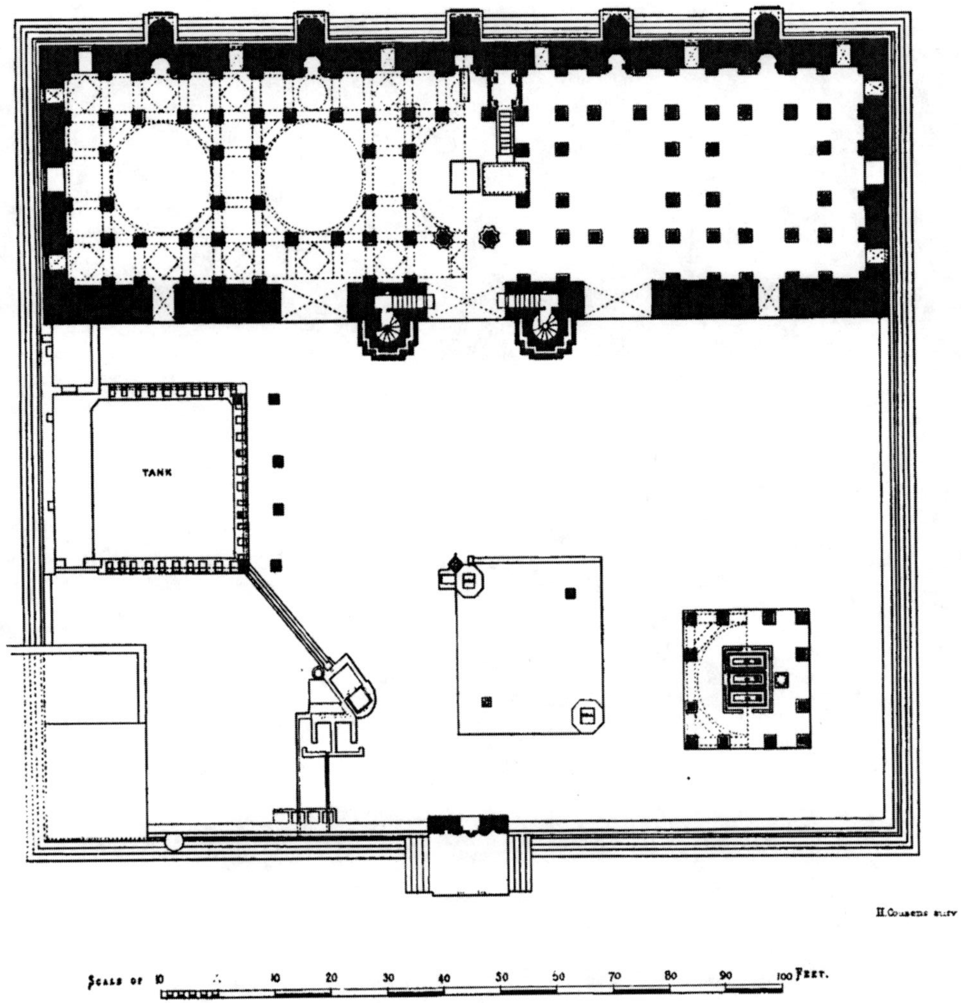

ḌHOLKÂ JÂMI' MASJID: WINDOW IN THE SOUTH END,

SCALE OF 12" — 1 — 2 — 3 — 4 — 5 FEET.

H. Cousens, surv.

PLATE LII.

ḌHOLKÁ : NICHE PANELS FROM THE MINARS OF THE JÂMI' MASJID.

NO. 1.

NO. 2.

H. Cousens. surv.

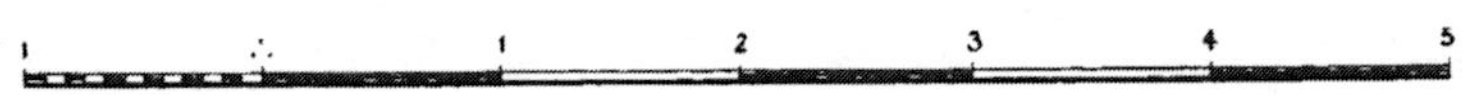

PLATE LIII.

ḌHOLKÂ: NICHE PANELS FROM THE MINARS OF THE JÂMI' MASJID.

NO. 3.

NO. 4.

H. Cousens, surv.

SCALE OF 1 ∴ 1 2 3 4 5 FEET.

ḌHOLKÁ: JÁMIʿ MASJID.

CENTRAL MIHRAB

FRONT ELEVATION

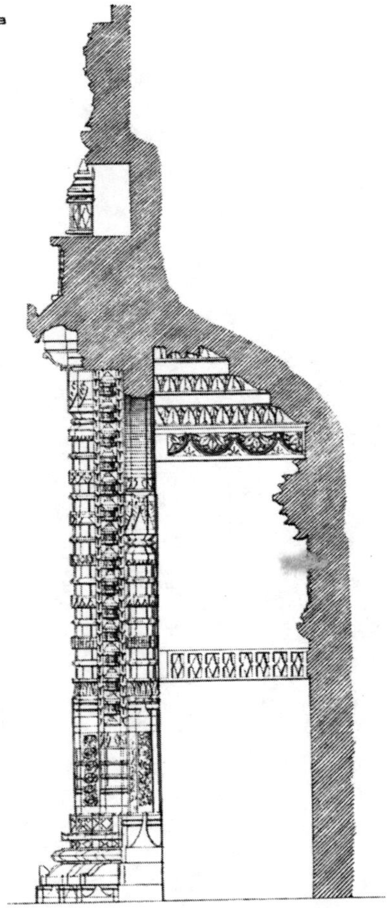

SECTION

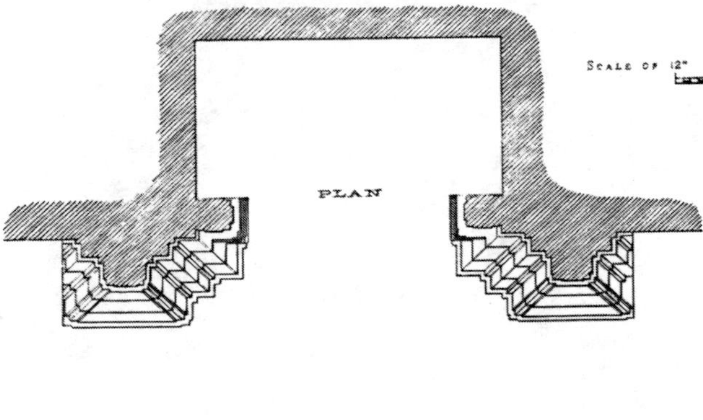

PLAN

SCALE OF 12" ∴ 1 2 3 4 5 FEET.

H Cousens. surv.

DHOLKA: HAZRAT KHAN'S TOMB AND ENCLOSURE.

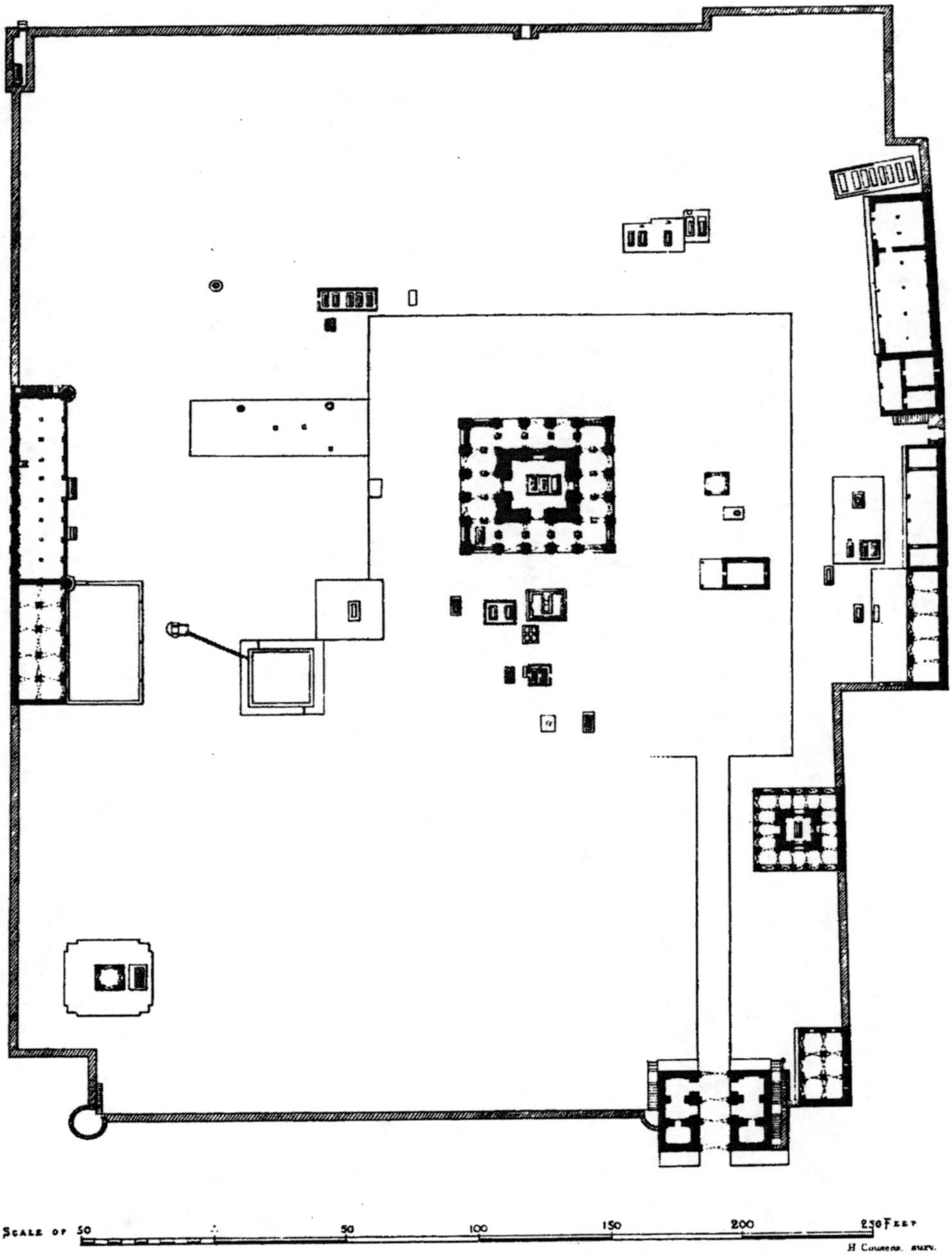

CHAPTER V.

CHAMPANIR.

CHÂMPÂNIR lies 78 miles south-east from Aḥmadâbâd in the Panch-Mahâls district, about twenty-five miles north-east of Baroda and twenty-two south of Godhrâ, the principal town of the district, and nearly a mile to the north-east of the main body of Pâwâgaḍh hill. That great isolated hill rises about 2,500 feet from the surrounding plain, and was a famous Hindû fortress under the Solaṅkhi kings of Gujarât. On the fall of the kingdom some of the Khichi Chauhâns made it (1297) their stronghold. By these Chauhans it was held for about 200 years. Early in the reign of Aḥmad Shâh I., Râja Trimbak Bhûpadâs of Châmpânir had, along with other Hindû chiefs, invited Sultan Hoshang of Mându to attack the Gujarât sovereign, and in 1418 Aḥmad Shâh invested Pâwâgaḍh, but was bought off by the chief. On his return from Mâlwâ in the following year he laid the territory of the chief utterly waste. Still the Râjâ was unsubdued, and in 1449, Muḥammad Shâh marched against the fort. Gaṅgâdâs, the son of Trimbakdâs offered resistance, but was forced to shut himself up in his fort, whence sending to Maḥmûd Khilji Sulṭân of Mându for aid, Muḥammad Shâh raised the siege.

After Maḥmûd Bîgarah had subdued Junâgaḍh in 1473, he sent an army to lay waste the Pâwâgaḍh or Châmpânir territory; and again, in 1482, a Gujarât officer led a plundering expedition into the same district, but it was boldly attacked by the chief Jaysingh Pâtâi Râwal and defeated with the loss of all the baggage. This roused Maḥmûd, and with a large force he marched against the fortress. At Baroda he was met with offers of reparation for the spoil taken and professions of allegiance, but answered that he would negotiate only with the sword. The place was invested; the chief appealed to Ghyâs ad-dîn of Mâlwâ for assistance, but after taking the field, the latter fearing what might be the result, again retired. The siege was pressed, and in their extremity, knowing too well the conduct of their Muslim enemies to the vanquished, they gave their women and children to the *johar*—a burning holocaust—and then rushed on their enemies, to be all slain. Râwal Pâthâi and his minister Dungarsî were taken wounded to the Sulṭân and urged to become Muslims.[1] They refused, and when their wounds were healed they were ordered to accept the creed of Islâm or death. On their again declining the chief's head was struck off and exposed on a gibbet.[2] Dungarsî, wresting a sword from a soldier killed one of the Sulṭân's connexions at a single blow, but was himself slain. The fort of Châmpânir was taken on the 24th (or 22nd) November 1484, and the Sulṭân renamed it Muḥammadâbâd.

The siege had lasted about eight and a half months, and Maḥmud, finding the climate agreeable, made a royal residence where his camp had been, and founded there

---

[1] *Râs Mâlâ*, vol. I. p. 373.

[2] A son of the Râwal—Pratapsingh—is said to have escaped to Hauf on the banks of the Narmadâ, and after many raids obtained the *chauth* of the revenues of Halol and Kalol. His grandson Trimbaksingh conquered Bâriya and divided his lands between his two sons who founded the Chhota Udaypur and Devagaḍh Bâriyâ chiefships.

a city which at first threatened almost to rival Aḥmadâbâd. It must have been of considerable extent, as in the beginning of the present century the ruins extended almost to Halol, about three and a half miles to the north-west.[1]

Maḥmudâbâd Châmpânir was the favourite residence of this sovereign till his death in 1511, and was, even till the death of Bahâdur Shâh in 1536, the political capital of Gujarât. It had fine streets and squares with houses of stone. In 1535 it was pillaged by the emperor Humâyun, and on Bahâdur Shâh's death in 1536, the court was transferred to Aḥmadâbâd, and its decline from this date was rapid.[2] By the middle of the seventeenth century so much of the country round it had lapsed into forest, that it was infested by tigers and was a hunting ground for wild elephants.

In the end of the eighteenth century it was seized by the Marâṭhas and finally fell into the hands of Mâdhavji Sindia. It was entirely neglected by his successor Daulat Râo Sindia, and on 17th September 1803, it was taken by the British; at that time half of the walled enclosure or citadel was occupied by silk and brocade weavers. In 1804 it was restored by the treaty of Serji Añjaṅgâon to Daulat Râo. In 1812 it contained about 200 inhabited houses, the people being chiefly runaways from Gujarât and a few silk weavers, but the latter were terribly thinned by cholera about 1828.[3] On July 31st, 1853, when it came under British management, the place was almost deserted. An attempt was made to bring in cultivators and clear the forest, but three fourths of the immigrants died and the rest fled. Latterly its only inhabitants are a few Kolis and Naikḍâs.

The citadel of Maḥmudâbâd Châmpânir is surrounded by a massive wall of freestone—the Jahânpanâh or 'world shelter.' "Enclosing an area about three-quarters of a mile long and two hunḍred and eighty yards broad, this wall, of great strength, and about thirty feet high, has at regular intervals bastions running north and east at right angles. Though much overgrown with creepers and clinging trees, the wall is in almost perfect repair. A few hundred yards from its western corner is the south or south-west gateway. At the entrance the line of wall falls back about 120 feet, and the road into the citadel lies between the two lines of wall through a rectangular building, probably a guard-room, about 150 feet long and 120 wide, with double gates, and in the south wall richly carved stone windows. On the inner gate is a Persian inscription of which the first figure of a date and the words 'Muẓaffar Shâh,[4] son of Maḥmûd Shâh' can still be read. Inside the citadel a little west of the gateway is the Shahr-ka Masjid or City Mosque, a beautiful building in fair repair. About 200 yards east and near the centre of the citadel is the Mândvi or custom house. This, probably used as a guard room, is highly finished, very simple and well proportioned. Nearly square, it is open at two ends, each open face having six bays and the two ends joined by five rows of arches, the whole forming a colonnaded chamber of five nearly equal aisles. The roof is flat and massive and though without ornaments, is much relieved on the inside. From the Mândvi

---

1 *Trans. Bom. Lit. Soc.*, vol. I. p. 141.

2 Stanley's *Barbosa*, p. 58; Bird's *Mirat-i-Ahmadi*, p. 233; Briggs's *Firishtah*, vol. IV. pp. 106, 133; *Bombay Lit. Soc. Trans.*, vol. II. p. 8; *Ind. Ant.*, VI. 2–8.

3 Hamilton's *Hindustan*, vol. I. p. 681; *Bom. Lit. Soc. Trans.*, vol. I. p. 145.

4 Reigned A.D. 1513–1526.

CHAMPANIR: FRONT OF THE JÂMI' MASJID.

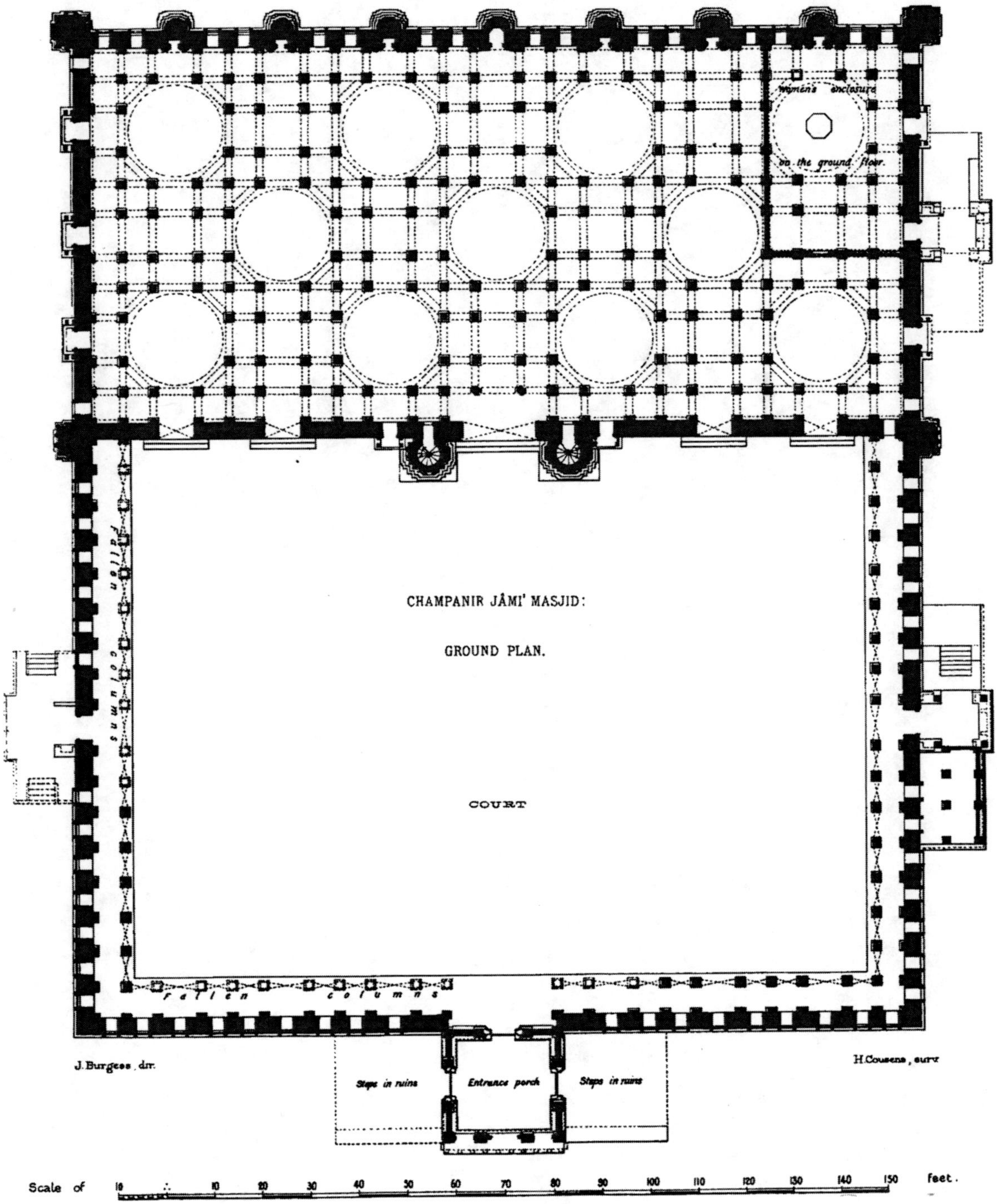

J. Burgess, dir.

H. Cousens, surv.

PLATE LVIII.

CHAMPANIR: JÂMI' MASJID FROM THE SOUTH WEST.

to the citadel's east gate stretches modern Châmpânir, a single street of mean huts. The east gate, built on the same plan as the south gate, equally massive, has the same inscription and the same guard room, only less ruined."[1]

The Jâmî' Masjid at Châmpânir.

The Jâmî' Masjid or Public Mosque stands about fifty yards from the east gate of Maḥmudâbâd Châmpânir. It is certainly one of the finest masjids in Gujarât. The minars rise from each side of the central and main entrance, to 100 feet in height. and the whole mosque is generally in excellent preservation, except that the top of the south minar is "shattered by a cannon shot wantonly fired at it by the tyrant Pâtankar, Sindiâ's governor in 1812."[2] (Plates LVI., LVII., and LVIII.)

Inside, the mosque measures 169½ feet by 81 feet. The pillars are so arranged as to provide for eleven larger domes—four along the front and back and three along the central line from north to south. With this plan, the pillars (exclusive of corresponding pilasters against the walls) run in ten rows from north to south and in twenty-two from east to west, but only four of the longitudinal rows and eight of the transverse ones are complete,—the others being interrupted for the domes. There are thus 172 pillars on the floor,—those rows which cross the domes being about 9 feet 3 inches between centres and the others nearly 6 feet 7 inches. As the pillars are 1 foot 6 inches square this gives an octagon 20 feet 10 inches in diameter to be covered by each dome. Between each pair of domes there will thus fall a space 7 feet 9 inches square, flanked by others 7 feet 9 inches by 5 feet 1 inch. These square spaces, ten in all, are covered by smaller domes. (Plates LVII. and LIX.)

The mosque has one main entrance, 15 feet wide, and four subordinate ones, each of half the width. The floor is about 2 feet above the level of the court, and the front wall at each end is about 23 feet high, with a projecting eaves-board or drip-stone, supported on carved brackets against a panelled frieze, over a string course carved with rozettes. Other two string courses—one at the spring of the arches of the doors, and another 5 feet lower—complete the decoration on the façades of these wing sections. The central portion of the façade, 51 feet in breadth, is raised to a height of 28 feet above the side wings, and against this wall the minârs are raised to about double its height. On the ground floor, outside the minârs on each side, is a projecting window supported on carved brackets, with side pillars, and over the great entrance is a similar window. Below this last and between the towers, is a bold projecting cornice. The minârs are elaborately carved in the style of the period up to the level of the vertex of the central doorway; and above this, at intervals, are carved cornices and decorative string courses. The stairs enter these minârs from within the mosque and lead up to the galleries, and to a door at the top of each tower.

On entering the main doorway, the first two pillars, rise to a height of 28 feet 10 inches, to support an upper floor over this inside porch, which is 21 feet wide by 12 feet deep. By this means the level of the general roof, which is only 17½ feet high,

---

[1] *Bombay Gazetteer*, vol. III. p. 308. [2] *Bombay Gazetteer*, vol. III. p. 309.

is carried back from the lofty entrance. The two pillars in this area are the only ones that have much carving upon them, and are represented on Plate LXV, fig. 1.[1] In the roof of the second storey just behind the heads of these pillars, the compartment is filled by a carved slab of great beauty and ingenuity of workmanship, which is represented in a photograph on Plate LXII.

About 16 feet behind this porch, and in the centre of the building is the one larger dome in this transverse line, and under this and its flanking areas, and up to the front wall, the structure is carried to a height of three storeys. Under this dome itself there are no floors, but a carved balcony runs round the octagon on the first and second floors, while at the spring of the dome is a deep and richly carved frieze (shown in the section, Plate LX.). The sixteen ribs of the dome are also neatly carved.

The two square corner compartments on each of the outer sides of this raised dome, are crowned by small domes,—the middle flanking areas being flat roofed. On the front side the roofs are carried forward to the façade wall (see also Plate LVIII.).

In the north-west corner of the masjid, an area about 45 feet by 28 on the floor, is, with one *miḥrâb,* enclosed by perforated stone screens about 9 feet high between the pillars, as a private chapel for the women. It is entered by a door in the centre of the north wall, and has an octagonal raised seat under the centre of the one dome over the area. There has been a porch outside with steps up to it on the north; but it is now quite ruined.

Including that in the women's enclosure there are seven *miḥrâbs* in the back wall corresponding to the domes, very similar to those in many of the masjids in Gujarât of the same age; the central one is somewhat more elaborate than the rest—and is given in plan, elevation and section on Plate LXI. In plan, it will be seen, it is a square with the inner corners cut off. It contained an inscription commemorative of the erection and containing a chronogram of the date of completion in the words:—

خطبه و منبر

—*Khuṭbah wa minbar* "The benediction and the pulpit"—in which the numerical values of the letters make 914, the Hijra year, corresponding to A.D. 1508–9. This tablet has now disappeared. Other two tablets contain usual verses from the *Qur'ân.*

In the back wall are sixteen perforated stone windows; in the south wall are two and in the north end two with projecting balconies, like those beside the minars. On the back wall outside behind each *miḥrâb* are the characteristic buttresses, so elaborately carved, and derived by the Gujarât workmen from the backs of Hindu temples. Then at the four corners are minarets, with a good deal of carving on the lower shafts, and rising 23 feet over the roof level (Plates LVIII. and LIX.).

The court in front measures 152 feet from north to south exclusive of the corridors and 115 feet from east to west, and is surrounded by a corridor open to the court and against an outer wall, with perforated lattice windows corresponding

[1] Through a mistake of the draftsman the scale to this figure is given as ¾-inch to a foot, instead of ½-inch, or half of the scale to figure 2.

[2] Briggs' *Firishtah,* vol. IV. p. 70.

CHAMPANIR JÂMI' MASJID: LONGIT

J Burgess dir.

Scale of 10 ∴ 10 20 30 40

PLATE LIX.

LONGITUDINAL SECTION.

H.Cousens, surv.

CHAMPANIR JÂMI' MASJID: SECTION OF THE CENTRAL DOME. PLATE LX.

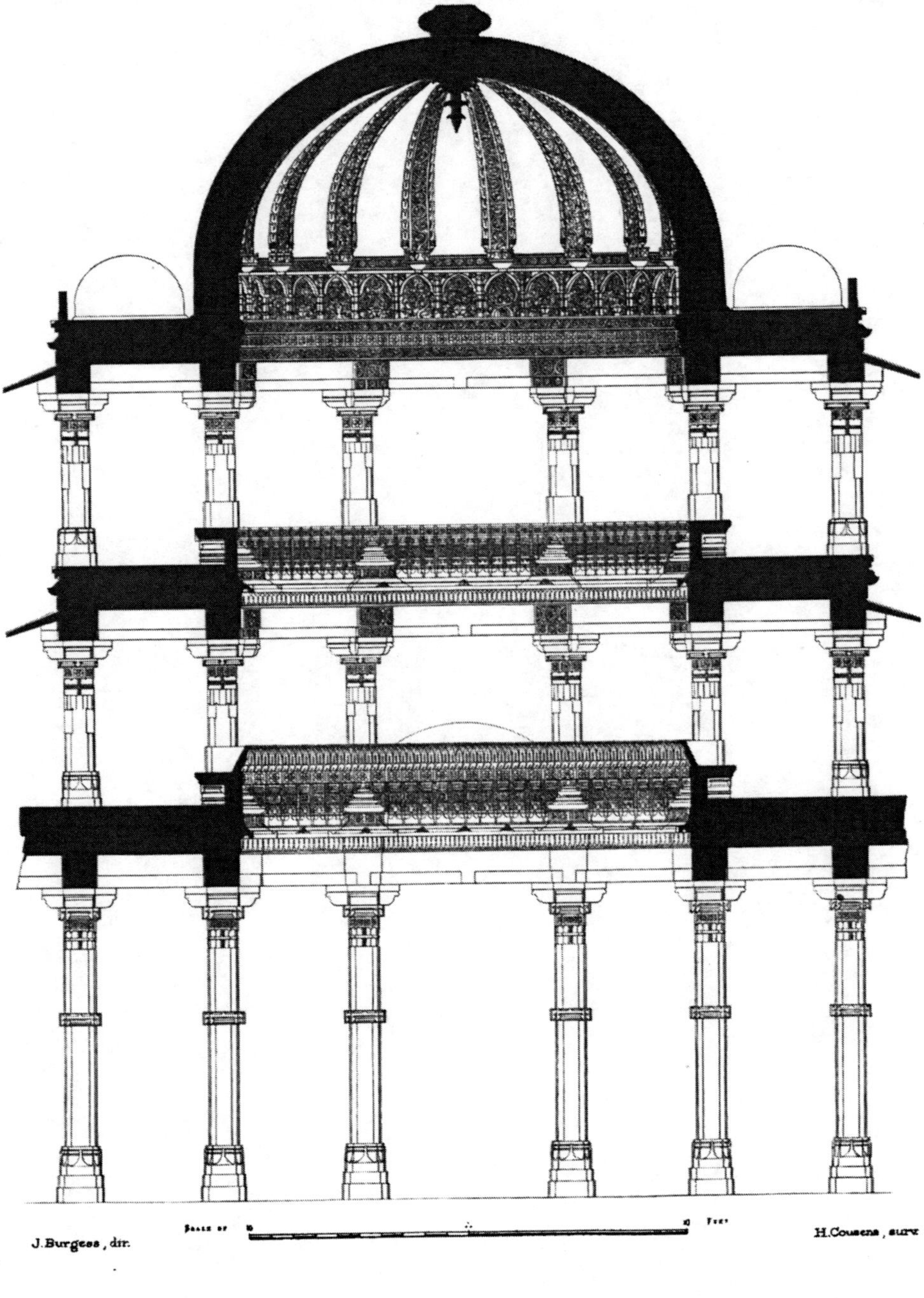

J. Burgess, dir.

H. Cousens, surv.

CHAMPANIR JÂMI' MASJID: CENTRAL MIHRAB. PLATE LXI.

J. Burgess. dir.

H. Cousens, surv.

CHAMPANIR JÁMI' MASJID: PANEL IN THE ROOF.

PLATE LXIII.

CHAMPANIR JÁMI' MASJID: COURT AND PORTICO FROM THE SOUTH EAST.

CHAMPANIR: DOOR OF THE EAST PORCH TO THE MASJID.

to the interspaces in the inner arcading (see Plate LXIII.). These windows are carved with every variety of patterns, and, as an example, one from the north wall is represented in the second figure on Plate LXV. Much of the corridor has now fallen in; the tank in the court has got filled up; and the area is occupied by large trees. In the middle of the north and south ends were porches leading to doors in the court wall. That on the south side is quite ruined; but on the north is in fair general preservation: It is approached by steps from the west, and has a sort of corridor to the east. The roof of this porch has been finished with much taste, and a carved panel from it is given on Plate LXV. But on the east or front, the porch was of unusual magnificence. Now it is sadly ruined, but the illustrations (Plates LXIII. and LXIV.) will convey some idea of what must have been its architectural merits when complete. It stood on a basement raised to the level of the court within, and was entered by doors on the north and south sides led up to by steps. On each side of these, and also over them were perforated stone windows. On the east was a projecting balcony—of which only the floor, supported by corbels, is left. Above were projecting eaves supported on brackets; the central area was covered with a brick dome raised on a moulded stone base, and at each corner was a small cupola supported on four pillars. Round the roof was a parapet of lattice work. The doorways were carved with a richness that can be best illustrated by the example of that on the north side given on Plate LXIV. Plate LXIII. shows this porch from the south, with a portion of the court wall.

Ruined Tomb.

As already stated, the whole site of Châmpânir has for long been all but entirely deserted, and the mosques and tombs have suffered by the destructive influences of climate and vegetation. Trees taking root in their roofs and domes and dislodging the stones till they fall down and the structures become ruins. Nor have they been left to such influences alone. The stones have been carried off for buildings and for road repairs.

Among those remains still found in the forest, attention may be drawn to the ruin of what must have been one of the most ornately carved tombs in Gujarât (Plate LXVI.). The dome has fallen in and the whole is a mere shell. It is not at all large, and had only one arched entrance on each side, with a blind arch on both sides of these entrances. The upper portions of these blind arches were ornamented with niches such as are common on the bases of minarets and by other rich carving; but the pilasters at the corners and jambs of the doorways are carved in patterns of the richest floral designs. Except the two famous windows in Sidi Sayyid's mosque at Aḥmadâbâd there is hardly anything elsewhere to match these twelve pillars in richness and variety of decoration. Sides of three of them are represented on Plate LXVII.

The base all round is carved in conventional patterns. A deep projecting drip-stone has been supported above by massive brackets, but the stones have all slipped from the brackets when the parapet above fell.

Nagîna Masjid at Châmpânir.

Some five or six hundred yards to the north of the citadel is the Nagîna or Jewel mosque, built of a very light—almost white—stone. It is somewhat on the plan of the Jâmî' Masjid but on a much smaller scale, having only one entrance on each side the main one. The central dome has fallen in, and the wall heads have been dismantled. The minars have two galleries above the line of the central façade, and the style and condition of the structure will be readily gathered from Plate LXVIII.

The lower portions of the minarets have been carved with much care and taste, and the niches are filled with floral designs as elegant and elaborate as any of those so often copied now-a-days in wood from the mosques of Aḥmadâbâd. One of these from the front of the north minaret and one from the south side of the other are represented on Plate LXIX.

In front of this mosque is another ruined tomb, from which the screens, that must have closed the spaces between the inner square of pillars, have entirely disappeared. It has six pillars on each of the four sides,—the central and outer pairs being farther apart than the second and third, and the fourth and fifth. The spandrels of the arches, in several cases, still contain the perforated panelling that once filled them all and at least the smaller arches, and most probably the corner arches also. On the west side is an advanced porch. The central area of the building was covered by a brick dome with bold projecting ribs, and the corner spaces were roofed by smaller ones of the usual plain type. The projecting eaves have mostly fallen—as was almost certain to occur where there was only a supporting bracket for each pillar of the corridor. Its general appearance will be best understood by a study of the photograph Plate LXX.

CHAMPANIR: DETAILS FROM THE JÂMI' MOSQUE.

PILLAR IN THE PORCH

Scale of 12 6 1 2 3 4 feet.

Scale of 12 6 1 2 3 feet.

WINDOW IN THE CORRIDOR OF THE COURT.

ROOF PANEL IN THE SOUTH ENTRANCE.

Scale of 12 6 1 2 feet

J. Burgess, dir.

H. Cousens, surv.

H. Cousens, surv.

CHAMPANIR: A RUINED TOMB.

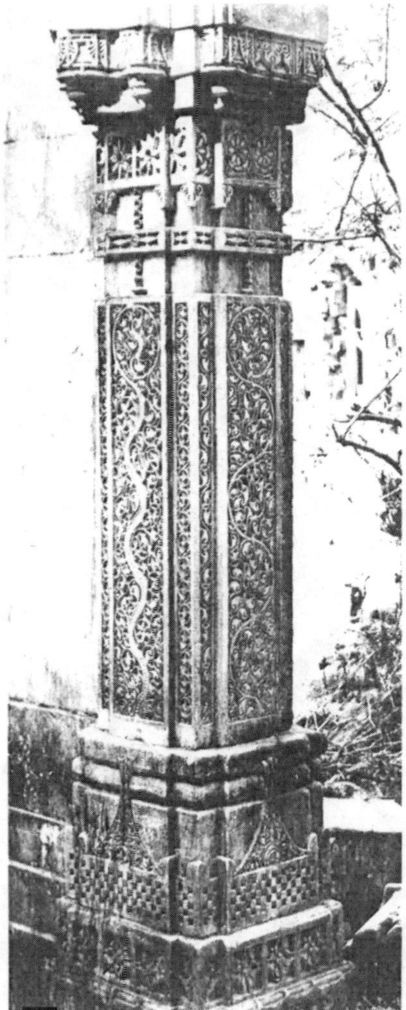

J Burgess, dir.

PILLARS FROM A RUINED TOMB AT CHAMPANIR.

J Burgess, dir. H. Cousens, photo

CHAMPANIR: NAGINA MASJID.

J Burgess, dir. H. Cousens, photo

CHAMPANIR: TWO NICHES IN THE MINARS OF NAGINA MASJID.

H. Cousens, surv

CHAMPANIR: A RUINED TOMB.

J Burgess, dir

PILLARS FROM A RUINED TOMB AT CHAMPANIR.

J Burgess, dir H. Cousens, photo

CHAMPANIR: NAGINA MASJID.

J Burgess, dir. H. Cousens, photo

CHAMPANIR: TWO NICHES IN THE MINARS OF NAGINA MASJID.

J. Burgess, dir. H. Cousens, photo

CHAMPANIR: LARGE RUINED TOMB.

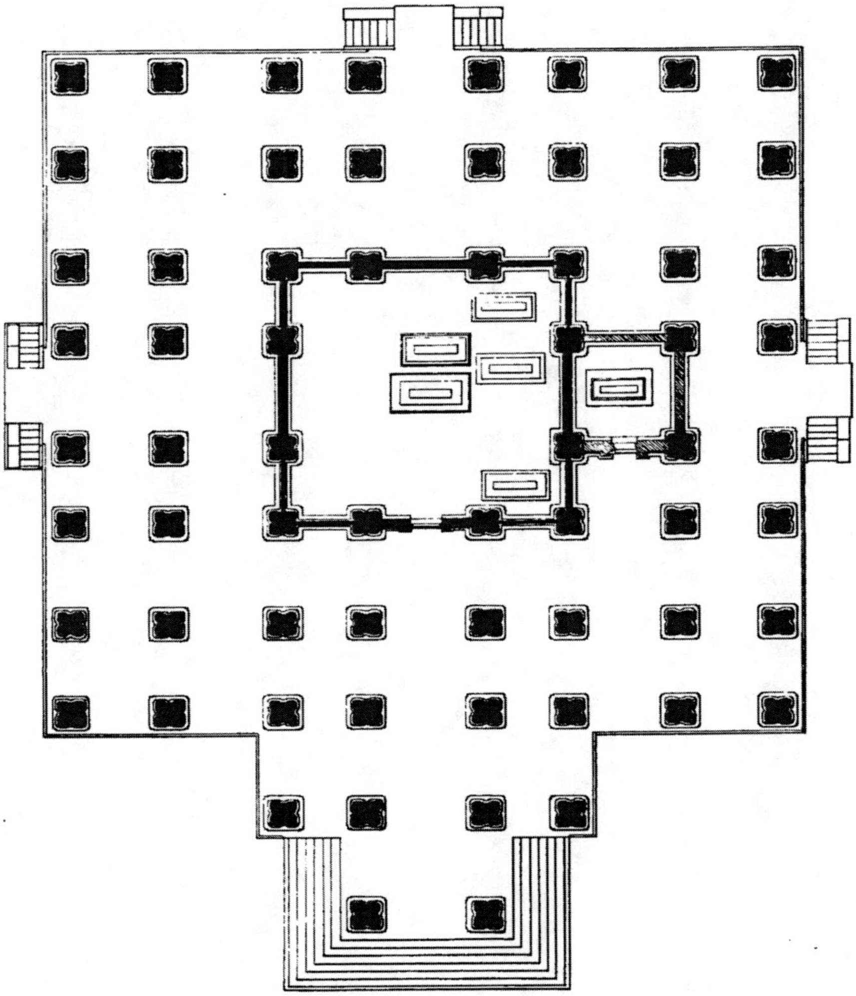

TOMB OF MUBARAK SAYYID, NEAR MAHMUDABAD: GROUND PLAN.

Scale of 10 ∴ 10 20 30 40 50 60 70 80 90 100 feet.

J. Burgess. dir

CHAPTER VI.

MEHMUDABAD.

MEHMUDÂBÂD or Maḥmûdâbâd is a considerable town in the Kheḍâ or Kaira district about seventeen miles south-south-east from Aḥmadâbâd, and on the railway to Bombay. It takes its name from Sulṭan Mahmûd Bîgarah who founded the city about 1479, and fortified it. Maḥmûd III. (1536–1554) formed beside it a large Deer park, five or six miles long, at each corner of which he built a pleasure house with gilded walls and roof. During the first half of the sixteenth century a great festival was celebrated here annually on the occasion of the birthday of Muḥammad, when the learned Muslim teachers rehearsed their traditions before the court.[1] In the seventeenth and eighteenth centuries the place fell into decay, but during the last half century it has greatly advanced in population and prosperity.

TOMB OF MUBÂRAK SAYYID.

About a mile and half east of the town, near the village of Sojâli is a small group of tombs belonging to about the end of the fifteenth century. The most important of these is the mausoleum of Mubârak Sayyid one of Maḥmûd Bîgarah's ministers, erected in 1484 (Plate I.). It stands on a platform 4 ft. 7 in. high and 95½ feet square, with an advanced porch on the east (Plate LXXI.). The pillars are massive and each is in the form of four square pillars grouped together. The innermost twelve piers forming a square, 36 feet between centres, are joined by perforated screens, and support the central dome. Outside these, which enclose the tomb proper, is a double corridor supported on thirty-six columns, with arches between each pier and roofed by small domes of various internal patterns (Plate LXXIII.). The piers have plain shafts with moulded bases carved with much taste and elegance, as is also the cornice of the podium or platform, which has also a string course running along at half its height ornamented with a very delicate floral pattern (Plate LXXV.).

The porch has four advanced pillars supporting small domes; and in front of these other two at the top of the steps, while over these and the two immediately behind them, a very neat little pavilion on twelve pillars, stands on the roof. The walls over the twelve central pillars are raised to form a square base for the principal dome, though inside the corners are also cut off by arches, for the support of the dome itself. Over the roof level are windows filled with perforated screens to admit light and air; and at a height of 38 ft. from the floor the dome proper begins. On the corners of its base are

---

[1] Bird's *Mirat-i Ahmadi*, pp. 212, 269; Gladwin's *Ain-i Akbari*, vol. II. p. 64; *Voy. de Olearius* (ed. Paris, 1659), tom. II. p. 133; Thevenot, *Voy.* vol. V. p. 97. The birthday of Muhammad is said to be the 10th of Rabi'u'l-Awwal; and he died on the 12th of the same month (A.H. 11) at the age of 63 lunar years and 2 days.

four little domed kiosks or pavilions, each with four pillars about 8 feet high. From the floor to the top of the inner curve of the dome is 57 feet; and from the ground level to the top of the finial is 70 feet. (See Plate LXXII.)

On the north, south, and east sides are steps by which to ascend to the platform; and, as already mentioned, the tomb, which is in the centre, is surrounded by screens of the most delicate perforated stone work. Most of these have been injured more or less, but much of the work is in fair preservation. That in the west end of the south face is given on Plate LXXIV. The inscription which will be remarked on the frieze, consists of extracts from the *Qur'ân;* there does not seem to be anywhere now a record of the builder or the date of the monument. Taken as a whole it is the most beautiful of these provincial examples—and "of its class one of the most beautiful in India." "There is," says Mr. Fergusson, "a simplicity about its plan, a solidity and balance of parts in the design, which is not always found in these tombs, and has rarely, if ever, been surpassed in any tomb in India. The details, too, are all elegant and appropriate, so that it only wants somewhat increased dimensions to rank among the very first of its class. Its constructive arrangements, too, are so perfect that no alteration in them would be required, if the scale had been very much increased."[1]

At the head or north side of the tomb four of the pillars have been enclosed to form a tomb for some one: but this is a comparatively modern addition. Three burials have also been made in the central chamber, beside (or rather at the head of) the two original interments of Mubârak Sayyid and his son Mîrân Sayyid.

To the south-west of this tomb are three smaller ones—one said to be that of the architect who built this tomb and that of Quṭb al 'Âlam at Batwâ, and the other two of Saif ad-dîn and Nizâm ad-dîn—brothers of Mîrân Sayyid's mother.

Bhamaria Well.

In Mehmudâbâd itself, there is a step-well of the usual construction, and probably of the fifteenth century. Outside, a little way from the town, on the way to Khaira or Kheḍa, is also the Bhamaria well, now in a very dirty and neglected state. Local tradition ascribes it to Maḥmûd Bîgarah, and this is probably correct enough. But when it is asserted that he made it for a hot weather retreat, and that the two stone arches over it were to hang the king's swing upon, we may reserve our full assent.

The well was probably in a pleasure garden, and is cut in the solid rock (Plates LXXVI., LXXVII.). The shaft is octagonal, about 14 feet across and over the mouth of it are two arches from east to west, which support lintels; and on these was placed the apparatus by which water was drawn up, and thrown into stone troughs on the north and west sides. On all four sides of the opening of the shaft were circular rooms—those east and west of 10 feet 8 inches diameter inside, and the other two 13 feet 3 inches diameter. Each of these was open to the shaft, and two of them had, in the openings, the troughs referred to. Outside, on the platform four stairs descended (as shown on Plate LXXVI.) to a lower storey,

[1] *Indian and Eastn. Archit.*, pp. 538, 539.

J Burgess, dir

H Cousens, surv

TOMB OF MUBARAK SAYYID: LONGITUDINAL SECTION.

J Burgess, dir

H Cousens, photo

TOMB OF MUBARAK SAYYID, NEAR MAHMUDABAD: THE CORRIDOR.

Scale of 12" 6" 1 2 3 4 5 feet.

J. Burgess, dir.

PERFORATED WINDOW IN MAHMUDABAD TOMB.

S. J. Pacheco, delt.

MAHMUDABAD TOMB: BASEMENT AND PILLAR BASE.

Scale of 12" 6" 0 1 2 3 4 5 feet

J. Burgess, dir.

OLD WELL, CUT IN THE ROCK, AT MAHMUDABAD.

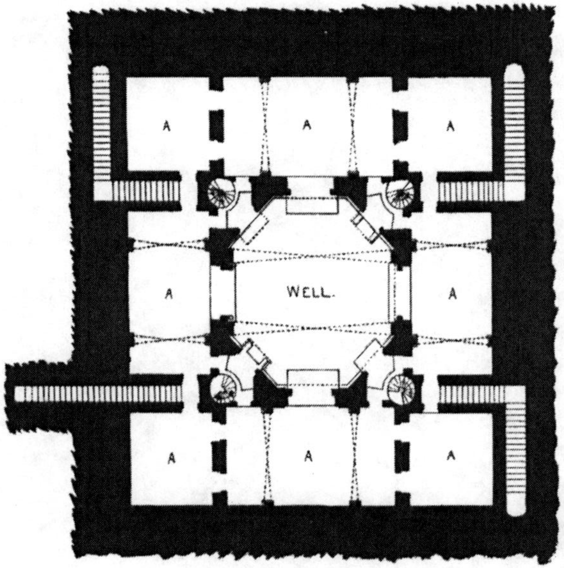

Plan of well and rooms below ground.

AAA &c. are small rooms around the shaft of the well below the ground level.
BB &c. are the foundations of circular walls at ground level.

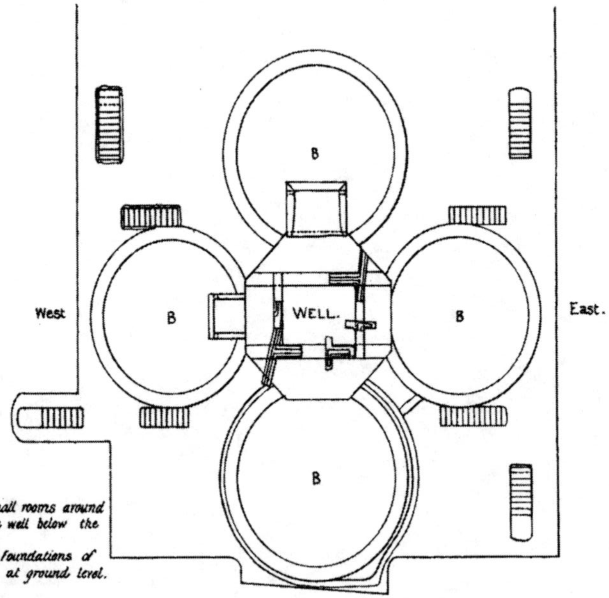

Plan above ground.

Scale of 10 … 10 20 30 40 50 feet.

J Burgess, dir.

H. Cousens, surv.

SECTION OF THE WELL AT MAHMUDABAD.

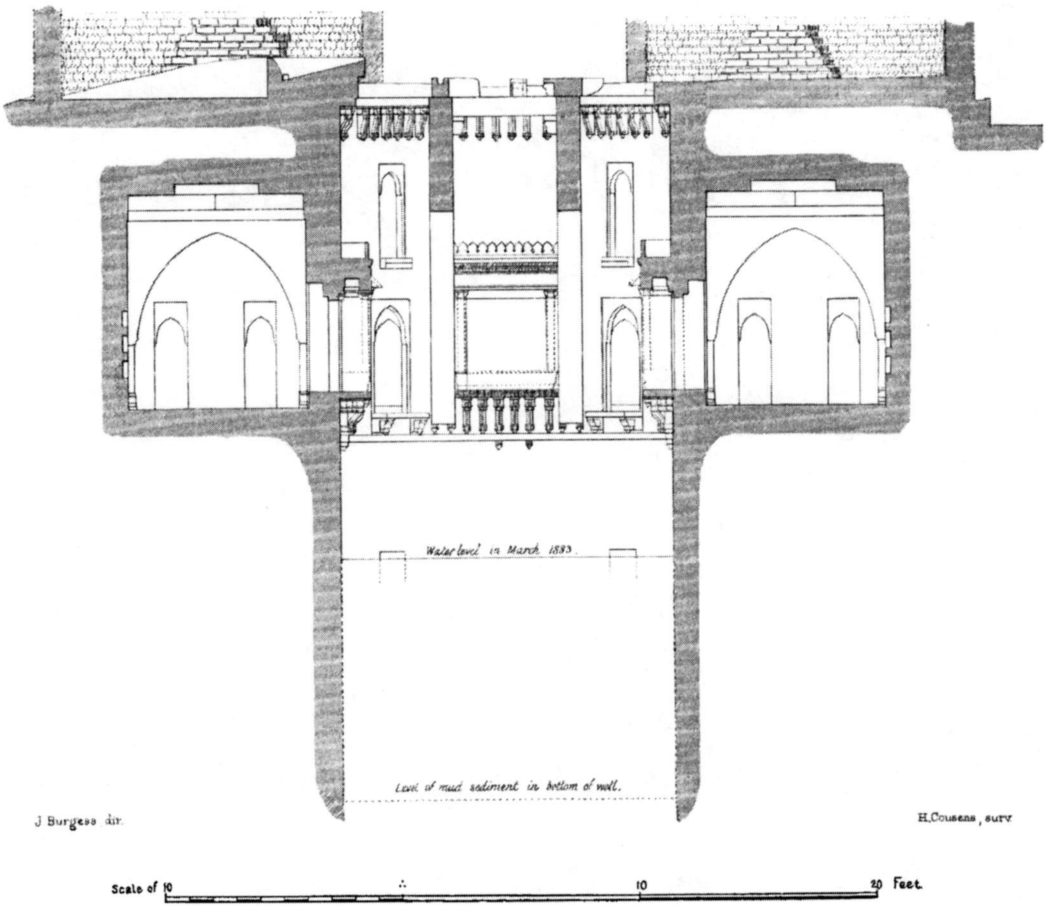

J Burgess dir.

H.Cousens, surv.

in which were eight rooms round the shaft: those in the corners each 8 feet square; two, east and west of the shaft each 12 feet 4 inches by 7 feet; and the other two 14 feet 7 inches by 7 feet 6 inches. These last four are each crossed by two Saracenic arches, and each has a neat balcony window into the shaft of the well (Plate LXXVII.).

So long as the water in the well was kept fresh, nothing could be cooler during the heat of the day in early summer than these rock-hewn chambers, and doubtless they were often occupied for an hour or two during seasons of recreation. In the other four sides of the octagon are narrow windows, arched above, and with projecting sills, and behind these are narrow spiral stairs descending to a lower storey, the tops of two narrow windows in which were just visible above the water, when the survey was made. But the water was so fœtid, no examination could be made below. The bottom is doubtless deeply silted, the mud standing up to about 27 feet from the well mouth. The section given on Plate LXXVII. is from north to south, cutting the main arches over the well, and is to double the scale of the two plans on Plate LXXVI.

List of Volumes constituting the New Imperial Series of the Reports of the Archæological Survey of India.

Prescribed Number in New Series.	Name of Book.	Author or Editor.	Date of Publication.	Existing Provincial Number.		
				Western India.	Southern India.	Northern India.
I.	Report of the first season's Operations in the Belgaum and Kaladgi Districts.	Burgess	1874	I.	—	—
II.	Report on the Antiquities of Kathiawar and Kachh.	Burgess	1876	II.	—	—
III.	Report on the Antiquities of the Bidar and Aurangabad Districts.	Burgess	1878	III.	—	—
IV.	The Buddhist Caves and their Inscriptions -	Burgess	1883	IV.	—	—
V.	The Caves of Elura and the other Brâhmanical and Jaina Caves in Western India.	Burgess	1884	V.	—	—
VI.	The Buddhist Stûpas of Amaravâti and Jaggayyapeta.	Burgess	1887	—	V.	—
VII.	Lists of Antiquarian Remains in the Presidency of Madras (Volume I.).	Sewell	1882	—	I.	—
VIII.	Lists of Inscriptions and Sketch of Dynasties of Southern India (Volume II.).	Sewell	1884	—	II.	—
IX.	South Indian Inscriptions (Volume I.) -	Hultzsch	1890	—	III.	—
X.	South Indian Inscriptions (Volume II.) -	Hultzsch	1891–92	—	IV.	—
XI.	Report on the Sharqi Architecture of Jaunpur	Burgess and Führer.	1889	—	—	I.
XII.	Monumental Antiquities and Inscriptions in the North-Western Provinces and Oudh.	Führer	1891	—	—	II.
XIII.	Epigraphia Indica (Volume I.) - -	Burgess	1891	—	—	—
XIV.	Epigraphia Indica (Volume II.) - -	Burgess	1894	—	—	—
XV.	South Indian Buddhist Antiquities - -	Rea	1894	—	VI.	—
XVI.	Revised Lists of Antiquarian Remains in the Bombay Presidency.	Cousens	Not yet published.	—	—	—
XVII.	Lists of Architectural and Archæological Remains in Coorg.	Rea	1894	—	VII.	—
XVIII.	Report on the Moghul Architecture of Fathpur-Sikri, Parts I and II.	Smith	1895–96	—	—	III.
,,	Fathpur-Sikri, Part III - - -	Smith	In press	—	—	III.
XIX.	Lists of Antiquarian Remains in the Central Provinces and Berars.	Cousens	Not yet published.	—	—	—
XX.	Monograph on Ancient Jaina Art and Architecture.	Führer	1896	—	—	IV.
XXI.	Chalukyan Architecture, including examples from the Bellary District, Madras Presidency.	Rea	1896	—	VIII.	—
XXII.	Bower Manuscripts - - -	Hœrnle	1894	—	—	—
XXIII.	The Muhammadan Architecture of Bharoch, Cambay, Ḍholkâ, Châmpânir, and Maḥmudâbâd, in Gujarât.	Burgess	1896	VI.	—	—
XXIV.	The Muhammadan Architecture of Ahmadâbâd.	Burgess	In preparation.	VII.	—	—

[EYRE AND SPOTTISWOODE, LONDON.—P. 5192.]

PRIVATELY PRINTED FOR SUBSCRIBERS ONLY.

THE RULERS OF INDIA
AND THE
CHIEFS OF RAJPUTANA,
1550—1895.

DEDICATED BY SPECIAL PERMISSION TO

Her Majesty the Queen-Empress.

The work will consist of a series of portraits of the Chiefs of Rajputana and of their ancestors as far back as the founder of each family, or the reign of Akbar, that is, for about 300 years.

The portraits will be careful reproductions in colour of originals which are in the possession of the Chiefs, and were the work, it is understood on good evidence, of contemporary artists in each case.

The Rajputana princes have, in most instances, shown considerable interest in the project, and have placed all their portraits at the disposal of Brigade-Surgeon Lieut.-Colonel Hendley, C.I.E., of Jeypore, the author of numerous works on Indian art, who will write the text for the book, and under whose supervision the portraits have been copied.

In order to make the work as complete as possible, it is proposed to include photographic reproductions of portraits of the British sovereigns from Queen Elizabeth, and of the Governors-General and Viceroys from Warren Hastings. The frontispiece will be reproduced from the Jubilee portrait of H.M. the Queen-Empress, who has been graciously pleased to accept the dedication of the book, and has also permitted the copying of miniatures and pictures of British sovereigns in the Royal Collections. The portraits of the Governors-General have been reproduced by kind permission of H.E. the Earl of Elgin, G.C.M.G., G.C.I.E., *the present Viceroy and Governor-General, from the paintings in Government House, Calcutta, which have never before been published.*

There will also be coloured portraits of the Moghul Emperors from Akbar to Bahadur Shah.

There will be in addition to the frontispiece (the portrait of Her Majesty the Queen-Empress), about two hundred portraits in colour on nineteen plates, and three or four collotype plates of portraits in monochrome of the British Sovereigns and Viceroys, as well as the descriptive matter. The whole will be handsomely bound, and form an edition de luxe *of special value to all who take an interest in the history of India and of its oldest families and in the noblest of its royal races.*

In 4to Imperial (size of "Journal of Indian Art and Industry").
Price to Subscribers, bound in cloth, £2 : 2 : 0; in morocco, £2 : 12 : 0.

WILL BE READY IN JUNE.

THE BUDDHIST CAVE-TEMPLES OF AJANTA. In two volumes. Edited by JOHN GRIFFITHS (late Principal of the School of Art, Bombay). With Map; 158 page plates, about half of which are in colours of originals; and text, with 88 cuts of details. Imperial folio (22 by 15 inches). Price of the two volumes, £10 : 10 : 0. Will be ready in April. Only a few copies remain for Subscribers in Europe.

DAMASCENING OF ARMS IN GOLD. A selection of the best examples, chiefly of sword hilts and dagger handles, with descriptive letterpress by Brigade Surgeon Lieut.-Colonel T. H. HENDLEY, C.I.E. The volume (Imperial quarto) contains Frontispiece, 105 examples of Damascening in 29 full-page coloured illustrations, and 2 plates of Tools. Price to subscribers, £2.

PHOTOGRAPHS OF THE ANCIENT MONUMENTS, TEMPLES, AND SCULPTURES OF INDIA. Published by subscription. The Secretary of State for India in Council has granted permission to use the very large collection of photographic negatives of Ancient Buildings, Sculptures, &c., from all parts of India, now in the possession of the India Office. These illustrate very fully the history and development of the various styles of Indian Architecture from the earliest times, in Buddhist, Brahmanical and Jaina Caves to Dravidian, Chalukyan, Indo-Aryan, and Saracenic temples, mosques, and other buildings. They constitute an indispensable series of illustrations of the art, history and mythology of India. A selection of 500 is in preparation in portfolio form, Imperial 4to (average size of picture, 8 in. by 10 in.), with brief letterpress description, £30. The portfolios will be issued in three divisions of about 167 plates, price £10 each. The plates have been selected by Dr. JAS. BURGESS, C.I.E., late Director General of the Archæological Survey of India. PART I. NOW READY. Lantern slides of this series will be prepared for lecture purposes; price £20 per set of 500.

JEYPORE PORTFOLIO OF ARCHITECTURAL DETAILS. Part VII, String and Band Patterns; Part VIII, Wall Decoration. Many of these are beautiful in design, and being drawn to scale, will be found most useful to decorators, workers in stone, metal, wood, or other material; also instructive to students in Technical and Art Schools, and interesting to all who appreciate native Indian art. Price £1 : 10 : 0 each part, with descriptive notes, in cloth portfolio complete. Only a few copies are retained for Subscribers in Europe.

INDIAN ART IN MARLBOROUGH HOUSE AND SANDRINGHAM HOUSE. By Sir GEORGE C. M. BIRDWOOD, K.C.I.E., containing 30 illustrations, mostly in colours. Imperial 4to, 10/-.

PORCELAIN TILES. A selection of eighteen patterns, in colours, of Porcelain Tiles from the Rauza of Mazai Sakhi; Musulla, Hirat; and the Shrine at Mazar-i-Sherif. Collected by the Afghan Boundary Commission, 1885. In portfolio, Imperial 4to, 10/-.

THE JOURNAL OF INDIAN ART AND INDUSTRY. Published quarterly. Richly illustrated with numerous plates in colour and gold, illustrative of the Arts, Architecture, Industries, and Manufactures of Hindustan. Containing Papers on Indian Gold, Silver, Copper, Brass, and other Metal Art Ware; Wood and Ivory Carving; Bidri Ware, Lacquer, Enamelling, Inlaid Work; Cloth Stamping and Dyeing; Bookbinding and Decoration; &c. Sent free by book post to any part of India or within the Postal Union, rolled solid, to those remitting 2/- for each part in advance.